Management Extra

MANAGING YOURSELF

ELSEVIER

eLEARN

Pergamon
Flexible
Learning

AMSTERDAM • BOSTON • HEIDELBERG • LONDON • NEW YORK • OXFORD • PARIS •
SAN DIEGO • SAN FRANCISCO • SINGAPORE • SYDNEY • TOKYO

Pergamon Flexible Learning is an imprint of Elsevier
Linacre House, Jordan Hill, Oxford OX2 8DP, UK
30 Corporate Drive, Suite 400, Burlington, MA 01803, USA

First published 2005
Revised edition 2009

British Library Cataloguing in Publication Data
A catalogue record for this book is available from the British Library

Library of Congress Cataloging-in-Publication Data
A catalog record for this book is available from the Library of Congress

ISBN 978-0-08-055745-8

For information on all Elsevier Butterworth-Heinemann publications
visit our website at www.elsevierdirect.com

Printed and bound in Hungary

Contents

Activities

Figures

Tables

Series preface

Whether you are a tutor/trainer or studying management development to further your career, Management Extra provides an exciting and flexible resource helping you to achieve your goals. The series is completely new and up-to-date, and has been written to harmonise with the 2004 national occupational standards in management and leadership. It has also been mapped to management qualifications, including the Institute of Leadership & Management's middle and senior management qualifications at Levels 5 and 7 respectively on the revised national framework.

For learners, coping with all the pressures of today's world, Management Extra offers you the flexibility to study at your own pace to fit around your professional and other commitments. Suddenly, you don't need a PC or to attend classes at a specific time – choose when and where to study to suit yourself! And, you will always have the complete workbook as a quick reference just when you need it.

For tutors/trainers, Management Extra provides an invaluable guide to what needs to be covered, and in what depth. It also allows learners who miss occasional sessions to 'catch up' by dipping into the series.

This series provides unrivalled support for all those involved in management development at middle and senior levels.

Reviews of Management Extra

I have utilised the Management Extra series for a number of Institute of Leadership and Management (ILM) Diploma in Management programmes. The series provides course tutors with the flexibility to run programmes in a variety of formats, from fully facilitated, using a choice of the titles as supporting information, to a tutorial based programme, where the complete series is provided for home study. These options also give course participants the flexibility to study in a manner which suits their personal circumstances. The content is interesting, thought provoking and up-to-date, and, as such, I would highly recommend the use of this series to suit a variety of individual and business needs.

Martin Davies BSc(Hons) MEd CEngMIMechE MCIPD FITOL FInstLM
Senior Lecturer, University of Wolverhampton Business School

At last, the complete set of books that make it all so clear and easy to follow for tutor and student. A must for all those taking middle/senior management training seriously.

Michael Crothers, ILM National Manager

Taking control of your life and work

This book is about managing yourself and your professional development. You will explore what you need to do to achieve your work objectives and your personal or career goals. Managing yourself means taking responsibility for various aspects of yourself: how you learn and understand, how aware you are of your actions, feelings and preferences, how you build self-discipline through managing your time and stress and how you balance your home and work lives.

The opportunity to change

This book introduces the ideas behind the wide range of tools and approaches you can draw on to improve the way you manage yourself. Overall these approaches make work easier to deal with and life in general more exciting. As well as personal benefits, self-management will strengthen relationships with colleagues and increase your effectiveness at work.

Your objectives are to:

♦ Take responsibility for your learning and planning your personal development

♦ Become more self-aware and understand your perspective on the world

♦ Identify ways of using your time more effectively and efficiently

♦ Find ways to manage your stress more effectively

♦ Plan your life to reduce home/work conflicts.

1   Learning and reflection

The fact that you are reading this suggests that you already value learning and see it as central to your own development. Increasingly, managers in all types of business are recognising that learning is crucial to their success. And this does not just mean the traditional, formal learning that may take place in a college, university or training room – it also involves learning at work. It is fair to say that today's effective manager is a learning manager.

We all learn in different ways. As a manager, you can try to be aware of your own learning strengths and preferences in order to make the most of your learning. You also need to be aware that individuals in your team may learn in different ways from you. This theme looks at learning preferences, styles and strategies.

One of the most important skills of the learning manager is the ability to learn from experience. But we don't automatically learn from our experiences – indeed many of our most fertile learning opportunities pass by without our making the most of them. The key to learning from experience lies in being able to reflect on what happens to us, and grasping the true meaning and message of the experience. We introduce the role of reflection in learning and highlight some practical ways of developing the skills of reflection.

This theme deals with learning and reflection. You will:

◆ **Review the importance of learning and reflection in the manager's role**

◆ **Identify factors that help to create a positive climate for learning**

◆ **Evaluate your learning preferences and how you can use them in practice to improve your performance at work**

◆ **Use strategies for improving reflective skills.**

The learning manager

Learning is crucial for today's manager for several reasons:

◆ **The pace of change.** Today's organisations face rapid change. When problems hit organisations today, they tend to do so much more frequently than ever before. New sources of competition, new forms of technology, new legal regulations, changing economic climates and employment patterns – all present organisations with new challenges and new opportunities. To cope, managers need to be quick on their feet. They need to be able to monitor the wider environment and anticipate change. All this calls for advanced learning skills.

◆ **The changing role of managers.** As organisations have evolved, so the role of the manager has changed dramatically over recent years. Gone are the days of the authoritarian enforcer of discipline. Today's manager has to be a leader, a motivator, a supporter and a coach to their team. This means not just being good at learning ourselves, but also knowing enough about how learning happens to help other people to learn effectively.

◆ **Changing career patterns.** Today's managers face very different career paths from earlier generations. The days when we could expect a job for life within a single organisation, with a clear, mapped-out career path, are long gone. Most people today expect to change jobs, organisations and even careers several times. This calls for continuous learning if managers are to remain employable.

◆ **Information overload.** The amount of information facing today's manager is colossal. Indeed, there is likely to be far more potentially relevant information than any of us can possibly cope with. Consequently, we need effective learning skills – especially the skills of being able to scan for, filter and digest information rapidly – in order to gain real value from the information explosion.

> **'The more you learn, the more you become aware of your ignorance.'**

All this has two important implications for you as a manager. First, it is important that your own learning skills are as good as possible. This involves recognising opportunities for learning and then learning effectively from them – whether during your work, through your reading, through your wider experience or through formal study. Second, it also makes sense to find ways to help your team learn effectively.

Learning organisations

It's not just managers who need to be good at learning, however. Many writers, including Charles Handy (1993), Rosabeth Moss Kanter (1989) and Tom Peters and Nancy Austin (1985), argue that learning is needed throughout the organisation if it is to adapt and thrive in today's changing world. Richard Schonberger, a leading writer on world-class organisations, comments that:

> All employees, from the CEO to bottom-scale new-hire, get on the path of continuous learning and don't ever get off.

Source: *Schonberger* (1990)

This awareness has led writers such as Bob Garratt to coin the term 'the learning organisation' to highlight this necessity for learning at all levels and in all parts of the organisation. Garratt argues that 'learning is central to the survival and growth of all organisations'. If any organisation is to survive and have a chance of growing, then:

> ...its rate of learning has to be equal to, or greater than, the rate of change in the external environment.

Source: *Garratt* (1990)

Garratt argues that it is vital for organisations to develop 'learning systems' that allow people to learn continuously. In particular, he describes ways in which managers can support learning in 'boss-generated' learning:

Garratt's 'Boss generated development'

Coaching, questioning and feedback. For Garratt, the 'learning leader' is someone who agrees targets with individuals and teams, delegates the authority to meet the targets, monitors and gives feedback.

Counselling. While coaching focuses on specific work, counselling applies similar processes to the whole person.

Mentoring. While coaching is the job of a line manager, there is also scope for managers to mentor people in other parts of the organisation.

Job rotation. Garratt argues that managers can help their people become multi-skilled and flexible by experiencing a range of jobs.

Source: *Garratt* (1990)

In his book *The Fifth Discipline*, Peter Senge suggests that a learning organisation requires five 'disciplines'.

Senge: Disciplines for a learning organisation

Senge identifies four core disciplines required to build a learning organisation:

1 **Personal mastery.** A high level of proficiency, which involves the individual in a commitment to their own lifelong learning, which in turn requires a commitment to learning by the organisation.

2 **Mental models.** Learning to unearth deeply ingrained assumptions and generalisations so we can expose our thinking effectively, and allow it to be open to the influence of others.

3 **Shared vision.** Unearthing shared 'pictures of the future' that foster genuine commitment.

4   **Team learning.** Results in the intelligence of the team exceeding that of the individuals.

When teams are truly learning, not only are they producing extraordinary results, but the individual members are growing more rapidly than could have occurred otherwise.

These four disciplines are integrated and given deeper meaning through the fifth discipline of:

5   **Systems thinking.** A method of thinking which draws our patterns, and helps us to see the effects of change.

All these disciplines involve lifelong learning – you never arrive, the more you learn the more you become aware of your ignorance.

Source: *Derived from Senge* (1990)

The climate for learning

If learning is so important for organisations, then how do we recognise an organisation where learning is likely to take place?

A positive climate for learning

In one recent piece of research, Eddy Knasel and John Meed identified a number of factors that appear to create a positive climate for learning in organisations. These include:

People are valued. Fundamental to the learning organisation is the way it sees its people. If the organisation sees its people as a disposable commodity, it is unlikely to place any great emphasis on learning. If, on the other hand, the organisation really values its people and genuinely wants them to grow and develop, then this will greatly enhance the climate of learning.

Learning has priority. One acid test of the learning climate is what happens when the organisation is under pressure. Does the organisation promptly cut the training budget or reduce the time that people have for learning? Or does the organisation believe that learning is a vital investment for the future, one that must continue?

There is an atmosphere of teamwork and support. People can learn on their own, but most people learn much better when they have support from their colleagues and manager. Effective team relationships appear to be key to the learning climate of any organisation.

People are prepared to admit and learn from mistakes. If an organisation has a 'blame culture' then people tend to mind their own backs and cover up their mistakes. The learning organisation recognises that mistakes happen and that they are opportunities to learn and prevent future mistakes.

People are encouraged to try out new approaches. A learning organisation appears to positively encourage people to experiment and create ideas.

Questions are encouraged. In the process of learning we pose questions and the learning organisation welcomes these from people throughout the organisation.

Everyone learns all the time. Finally, people recognise that learning is something that happens all the time, whenever the opportunity arises – not just in formal training and educational contexts.

Source: *Knasel and Meed* (1994)

Activity 1
Assess the learning climate in your organisation

Objective

Use this activity to assess the learning climate in your organisation.

A positive learning climate is one that stimulates, encourages and supports learning.

Task

1 Score your organisation against each of the aspects of a positive learning climate in the grid which follows. Choose a score from 1–5. If your organisation scores very well on an aspect, give it 5 points; if it does badly, give it 1 point; and so on.

2 In the comments column add brief notes and/or examples explaining why you have given the organisation this score.

Aspect of the learning climate	Score (1–5) where 5 is positive and 1 is negative	Comments
People are valued	□ □ □ □ □ 1 2 3 4 5	
Learning has priority	□ □ □ □ □ 1 2 3 4 5	
There is an atmosphere of teamwork and support	□ □ □ □ □ 1 2 3 4 5	
People are prepared to admit and learn from mistakes	□ □ □ □ □ 1 2 3 4 5	
People are encouraged to try out new approaches	□ □ □ □ □ 1 2 3 4 5	
Questions are encouraged	□ □ □ □ □ 1 2 3 4 5	
Everyone learns, all the time	□ □ □ □ □ 1 2 3 4 5	

Feedback

Discuss your findings with your colleagues. Do you share the same views? What are the effects of the climate? What improvements could be made?

Ways of learning

Much of the early research into learning focused on the best ways of teaching a topic. Writers such as Gagné (1985) looked at how it was possible to 'create conditions for learning' which would ensure that people could learn a subject effectively. These ideas have been very influential for people who design learning.

Useful as such ideas can be, however, they do not give the whole story. A number of writers and researchers moved the focus away from how a topic is taught and on to how individuals learn. In the process they have made some important discoveries:

◆ First, it has become clear that people have different preferences and styles of learning. For example, while one person may like to learn in a group, with lots of social contact, someone else may prefer to study alone, mulling things over in their own time.

◆ Second, some important research with students has shown that people can adopt very different approaches or strategies for learning. These contrasting strategies can have an important impact on how well they master and remember what they learn.

These discoveries have some very practical benefits for managers. They give important insights into how you – and the people in your team – learn best. They also give some pointers towards how we may be able to learn better.

Models of learning styles and strategies

Several writers have researched and identified different learning styles and strategies. One of the most well-known models in training and management was developed by Honey and Mumford.

Honey and Mumford's model of learning styles

Peter Honey and Alan Mumford have identified four different learning styles:

◆ **Activists** readily embrace new experiences

◆ **Reflectors** would rather consider all the information before acting

◆ **Theorists** like to understand the general principles underlying things

◆ **Pragmatists** test out new ideas in practice.

Different styles have their own strengths and an individual manager may be able to adopt different styles for different contexts.

Source: *Honey and Mumford* (1976)

An alternative model of learning styles focuses on the way in which we take in information. This model proposes three different styles:

- The **kinaesthetic** style – people who prefer this style tend to prefer learning in a practical, hands-on way
- The **visual** style – other people may be particularly strong at learning from visual stimuli
- The **oral** style – finally, some people may prefer to learn by speaking and listening.

These models can give us some useful insights into our learning preferences. However, the work of writers like Gordon Pask goes a step further. Pask argues, for instance, that people adopt contrasting strategies for learning that may have a real impact on how effectively they learn.

Gordon Pask's model of learning strategies

Gordon Pask argues that the research highlights contrasting learning strategies or approaches:

- The **holistic** approach (also known as 'deep' or 'comprehension' learning) involves a search for meaning and understanding. The holist tends to make more elaborate hypotheses, look further ahead and build up a picture of the whole task.
- The **serialist** approach (also known as 'surface' or 'operation' learning) involves an emphasis on memorising. The serialist prefers a narrower focus in learning – concentrating on simple hypotheses and step-by-step learning and paying greater attention to detail, but neglecting the broader links.

Pask argues that both approaches have their strengths and weaknesses. He suggests that 'students who adopt a holistic approach...find their work more interesting and rewarding – in terms of both personal satisfaction and higher grades' than serialists. Pask claims that 'versatile' learners are able to use both holistic and serialist strategies as appropriate and in effective sequence.

There is some evidence to suggest that there can be real benefits from adopting a 'holistic' or 'deep' approach to learning – and above all from being able to adopt different approaches in different contexts. For example, if you are using a computer manual to learn how to use a particular piece of software, a surface approach may be appropriate. On the other hand, if you are doing some strategic planning, it is helpful to see the bigger picture by adopting the holistic approach.

Source: *Pask* (1988)

Issues around labelling

There are, however, some downsides to using learning styles. Above all, there is a risk of labelling yourself or others as 'activist', 'visualist' or 'serialist'. Doing this can severely damage your learning because it can restrict the range of styles and approaches available. There are indeed several reasons why you should avoid labelling yourself with a particular style:

- ◆ The importance of versatility – there appear to be clear advantages to adopting a range of styles and approaches in different contexts, rather than sticking with a single style and approach
- ◆ A lack of consensus – there are concerns about the reliability of typologies of learning styles
- ◆ Your self-knowledge is at least as important as your preferences for particular styles.

Source: *Knasel et al.* (2000)

Labelling is an issue in other areas as well – see, for example, personality types in the section *The importance of self-awareness*.

Becoming a competent learner

All this suggests that effective learners have a good awareness of learning styles and are able to adopt different approaches in different contexts. There are several practical steps that you can take to make the most of your learning:

- ◆ Get to know yourself by reflecting on your experiences of learning. What have you most enjoyed learning?
- ◆ Reflect on the things that have helped you to learn in the past. In particular, have other people helped you?
- ◆ Experiment with approaches you have not used before. Could you try learning in a self-help group, for example?
- ◆ Talk to other people about how they learn. Do they have any techniques or approaches that you could try out?
- ◆ Try out one or more of the learning style questionnaires.

Activity 2
Analyse your past learning

Objective

Use this activity to analyse your past experiences of learning.

We are all influenced by our past experiences of learning – at school and elsewhere. Reflecting on these experiences can help us to identify our learning strengths and plan our future learning.

Task

1 Choose two things that you have learned in the past:

◆ One that you enjoyed learning and/or found positive

◆ One that you did not enjoy learning and/or found negative.

These could be things you learned at work, school, college or indeed in any aspect of your life.

2 Briefly describe the experience in each case.

3 Analyse why each experience was positive or negative.

The experience	Description	Analyse
A learning experience that you enjoyed and/or found positive		
A learning experience that you did not enjoy and/or found negative		

4 In the light of your analysis, what conclusions can you draw about your learning strengths? Note down your thoughts here.

Conclusions:

Feedback

Your work on this activity should have given you some ideas about your learning strengths. You should be able to draw on these in your future learning, for example when you need to:

◆ choose a method of learning

◆ choose who you will learn with

◆ decide when you will learn.

Activity 3
Broaden your learning style and strategies

Objective

Now use this activity to:

◆ examine your own learning preferences

◆ experiment with new approaches.

We all have our own preferences about how to learn. It is useful to know what these preferences are, and to consider adopting a range of styles and approaches to learning.

Task

1 Begin by thinking about whether you prefer working with or without other people. Decide whether you agree or disagree with each of the following statements, and tick the appropriate box.

Agree		Disagree
☐	I like to learn in a group	☐
☐	I like to learn one-to-one with another person	☐
☐	I enjoy learning on my own	

2 Then go on to think about how you take on board new information. Again, tick the appropriate box for each of these statements.

Agree		Disagree
☐	I enjoy going for new experiences	☐
☐	I like to have time to reflect on information before acting on it	☐
☐	I like to understand the general principles underlying things	☐
☐	I like to test out new ideas in practice	☐

3 Next, consider whether you prefer learning in visual, oral or practical ways.

Agree		Disagree
☐	I learn best by looking and seeing	☐
☐	I learn best by listening and speaking	☐
☐	I learn best by doing practical things	☐

4 Finally, consider how you approach learning. Which of the following statements is true for you?

Agree		Disagree
☐	I like to learn new things in a step-by-step way	☐
☐	I like to stand back and form an impression of the big picture	☐
☐	I like to focus on the detail	☐
☐	I like to make links between different ideas	☐
☐	I like to work with simple hypotheses	☐
☐	I enjoy working with elaborate hypotheses	☐

Feedback

This activity has looked briefly at some of the elements of learning styles and approaches. However, you should already be able to make some use of your responses to these questions:

1   Look at those statements that you agreed with. Ask yourself why you ticked these. For example, if you said you liked learning in a group, is this because you enjoy the social interaction? Because you like discussing other people's ideas? Or because you can listen without taking a very active part?

2   Then look at those statements you disagreed with. Select two or three of these that you might like to try out when next you have to learn something.

3   You may like to try some of the more detailed learning style questionnaires to find out more about how you learn.

4   Consider what you can do as a result of 1–3.
    Write your ideas here:

Action to take

The reflective practitioner

Reflection is central to learning for several reasons. First – and crucially – it is part of learning from experience. The writer David Kolb is famous for his model of learning from experience, often referred to as the Kolb cycle. He argues that reflection is a vital stage in the learning process. We reflect on our practical, concrete experience in order to build up our own ideas – our picture of the world – which we then test in new situations.

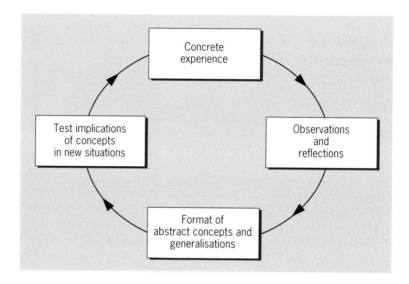

Figure 1.1 *Kolb's model of learning from experience*   Source: *Kolb* (1984)

Second, reflection can help us to work out how other people's ideas and theories may work in practice. For example, as well as reading about the ideas on learning in this book, it is also important to test them out in your own work. The activities associated with this theme will help you to put the ideas into practice.

Third, reflecting on our work can help us to question why we are doing things, and whether we are doing them the right way. As Mary Fitzgerald (1994) has suggested, reflection can enable us 'to critically analyse and interpret' what we do.

Reflective skills are becoming ever more important for today's managers, given the increasing pace of change and the accompanying levels of stress and uncertainty we must deal with. Being able to reflect on the problems we encounter gives us a much better chance to find solutions.

Donald Schön: The reflective practitioner

Donald Schön is possibly the most influential writer on reflection. Schön researched the ways in which people in different professions, including managers, architects and doctors, go about solving the complex problems they encounter in their work. He found that they were able to learn in a highly sophisticated manner by applying the skills of reflection.

Schön argues that an important element of reflection is experimentation. In effect, when confronted with a problem, we create a hypothesis to explain the problem. We then test this out to check whether our hypothesis was right, and if necessary, adapt and change the hypothesis.

Schön makes a distinction between what he calls 'reflection-on-action', when we take time after an event to reflect on what happened, and 'reflection-in-action', when we are able to reflect during an activity. He claims that as professionals become more experienced, they are able to move increasingly from 'reflection-on-action' to 'reflection-in-action'. See his example of reflection-in-action below.

Reflection-in-action

Schön describes how an eye specialist was confronted with a patient who had two eye conditions at the same time – an inflammation and a glaucoma – both of which appeared to be getting worse. The specialist had never met this combination of conditions before, and was initially puzzled about what to do. After initial reflection, he hypothesised that the treatment for each condition was aggravating the other condition. He conducted an experiment to test this out by temporarily withholding all treatments to see what effect this would have. As a result the glaucoma disappeared, proving the hypothesis that it was caused by the treatment for the inflammation. The specialist was then able to consider other ways of treating the inflammation.

Source: *Schön* (1983)

Patricia Benner: Becoming expert

Another influential writer on reflection is Patricia Benner, who studied the ways in which nurses learn their professional skills. She found that while newly qualified nurses may have learnt important skills and knowledge, it will take several years of learning both at and away from work before they become truly expert. Benner argues that several things mark out the expert from the novice:

◆ Experts are able to draw on their own experience of work

◆ They can quickly build a picture of the whole problem, and recognise which aspects may be most important

◆ They use intuition to understand their clients.

◆ Recap

This theme has explored learning and reflection.

Review the importance of learning and reflection in the manager's role
Learning is crucial for managers today because of the pace of change, changing roles and new career patterns. We also have a vastly increased pool of knowledge through which we need to be able to sort.

Identify factors that help to create a positive climate for learning
The factors that contribute to a positive climate for learning include valuing people, giving learning a priority, promoting teamworking and support, learning from mistakes, trying out new approaches, questioning and lifelong learning.

Evaluate your learning preferences and how you can use them in practice to improve your performance at work
Evaluating learning preferences is an important tool to help support learning and learners. We can improve performance if we recognise that people learn in different ways and adopt different approaches in different contexts.

Use strategies for improving reflective skills
Reflection is central to learning from experience and for the application of theory to practice. The reflective diary is designed to help you highlight your use of reflective learning.

▶▶ More @

Kolb, D. A. (1984) *Experiential Learning: Experience as a Source of Learning and Development*, Prentice Hall
This is a seminal text on the structure and process of learning by experience. It covers individuality in learning and learning styles, the structure of knowledge and the theory of development. Kolb is still influential in all areas of learning and development.

Pedler, M., Burgoyne J. and Boydell T. (1996) *The Learning Company*, McGraw-Hill
This text provides tools such as a 'Learning Company' questionnaire and offers examples to design and create an organisation that is capable of adapting, changing and developing. A new 'Reflections' section covers IT, computer networks, organisational development writers and organisational ecology.

Senge P. M. (1990) *The Fifth Discipline*, **Century Business**
A fascinating text in which the author defines five business
'disciplines' which help to build 'learning organisations'. These
companies will be the successful ones in the coming decade because
of their ability to learn, to absorb new ideas, theories and practices
at all employee levels and use them to competitive advantage.

www.peterhoney.com/product/brochure
The manual of learning styles, **Peter Honey Publications**
You can access a whole range of resources on learning styles and
their application in the workplace from this website.

www.astd.org/astd/Research/research_reports.htm
For more general information and some excellent articles explore
the **American Society for Training and Development** for the latest
on learning theory at work.

Full references are provided at the end of the book.

2 Personal development and self-awareness

The changing world of work has had a significant impact on the roles and career paths of managers. As a manager you are likely to have to take a fair amount of responsibility for your own development. You will do so within the context of some uncertainty, where your own role within the organisation, and your wider career, may appear unpredictable. This theme looks at how you can plan your own development to take account of an unpredictable future.

Managers also have to be good at understanding people and what makes them tick. It is important to get to know the individual members of your team, and to understand what matters to them. As a starting point, however, you above all need to know yourself. Here we look at why self-awareness is important for managers, and the ways in which it may impact on your team.

This theme asks you to plan your own development and examine what makes you tick. You will:

◆ **Examine the impact of changing career patterns on personal development**

◆ **Consider your career path and personal objectives**

◆ **Plan your professional development to aquire the skills and knowledge your will require in the future**

◆ **Use a range of approaches to explore your values and performance.**

Planning your own development

Thirty years ago it was commonplace to spend an entire working life in a single organisation. The training and development undertaken at the start of their careers would last people for much of their lives.

All this has changed. It is now common for people to change jobs, organisations and indeed careers – in some cases several times – in the course of their working lives. Writers such as Edgar Schein (1970) and Charles Handy (1991) talk about the changing nature of the 'psychological contract' – some organisations now say they will commit to keeping their employees employable, rather than employing them for life.

It is therefore not surprising that writers in the field have fundamentally reconsidered what career planning and development mean today.

New ideas in personal development

One of the most influential writers on the changing world of work is Charles Handy. In his book *The Age of Unreason* (1991), Handy argues that developments such as information technology, telecommunications, genetic engineering and biotechnology are leading to radical changes in employment patterns. He points out that many organisations are now organised around a small core of full-time employees, with much work sub-contracted to suppliers.

Charles Handy: The portfolio career

For Handy, thanks to the reshaping of organisations, we shall all be 'portfolio people', that is, we will increasingly take on a range of activities – some paid and some unpaid – which add up to the equivalent of a traditional job. For Handy the secret of a portfolio career is in finding out what you are good at and which of your skills are most reliable.

Source: *Handy* (1991)

Other writers have explored ways in which changing generations view their development. Jay Conger, Professor of Organisational Behaviour at London Business School, has explored the idea of 'Generation X' managers – people born between 1965 and 1981.

Jay Conger: Generation X

For Conger, the Generation X managers differ from their baby boomer predecessors in several ways. They are technologically literate and enthusiastic, collaborative and able to work in teams, concerned with achieving a work/life balance, direct communicators, independent and self-reliant. They tend to be loyal to their professions rather than to their organisations, which is not surprising in an age of downsizing and flexible working. They prefer to work in organisations structured as communities, rather than hierarchical models – for example, the college campus ideas of organisational structures at Nike and Microsoft.

Source: *Conger* (1998)

> **Bill Law: Career learning**
>
> Another writer on career management, Bill Law, has coined the term 'career learning'. Law argues that 'people need to review career choices and transitions, with thought and care'. Through career learning, people can learn to manage their careers in an active, dynamic way that takes account of the unexpected, uncertain nature of modern work.

Source: *Law* (1996)

The implications for personal development

These changes have several implications for your own personal development. You are likely to have greater freedom and choice over what you do with your time. You can consider blending work with other activities, taking breaks during your career, etc. All this would have been much more difficult in the past. The other side of this equation is that you will need to deal with greater levels of uncertainty and unpredictability in your career. Redundancy can hit anyone today at any time; equally, new opportunities may arise that you have not foreseen. This means taking stock of where you are and where you are going on a regular basis, building the skills to reflect on your career. When you do this, you may need to revisit your life goals and possibly readjust your horizons.

You will need a personal programme of continuous development if you are to keep abreast of changes and ensure you have the skills and knowledge you need to achieve your goals. This will call for continual learning.

Consider how you will market yourself. The leading writer on management, Tom Peters, has suggested that everybody needs a 'personal brand' if they are to make the most of their skills and experience.

> **Tom Peters: The brand called You**
>
> Tom Peters argues that 'to be in business today, our most important job is to be head marketer for the brand called You'. Peters claims that everyone needs to begin by working out which are their distinctive characteristics and personal strengths – this might include working well in a team, being good at meeting deadlines, etc. They then need to find ways of presenting these, both within their existing work and in other contexts.
>
> Peters argues that 'everyone has a chance to stand out. Everyone has a chance to learn, improve and build up their skills.'

Source: *Peters* (1997)

Planning your own development

All this calls for a dynamic approach to planning your own development. In their book *The Learning Company* (1991), Mike Pedler, John Burgoyne and Tom Boydell argue that everyone should have a personal development plan which they review and update regularly.

Pedler, Burgoyne and Boydell: A three-part personal development plan

Pedler et al. argue that personal development plans can help to 'direct ourselves towards desired ends – towards becoming the person and professional we want to be'. They suggest that there are three key stages in creating a personal development plan:

Part 1: Preparation. This involves asking yourself a series of questions about your current job, your career interests and your development needs in order to think through your needs and ambitions.

Part 2: Development plan. This involves setting goals for development, target dates and methods of achieving the goals.

Part 3: Action plan. This involves identifying what to do to achieve your plan, who can help, when you will review the plan, and so on.

Source: *Pedler et al.* (1991)

Planning personal development involves:

- reflecting on your goals
- identifying development needs
- deciding how you will learn
- action planning – who, where and when.

The activities at the end of this section provide an opportunity for you to examine your career and then plan your development against this framework.

Reflecting on your goals

The first step in planning your personal development is to reflect on your goals. These will include both your work goals – what you want to achieve in your job – and your other life goals – things you want to achieve in your relationships, your leisure interests, and so on. Examples of goals might include:

- completing a challenging project
- gaining a specific qualification
- learning to play a musical instrument.

See the section *Balancing home and work* for more on life and work goals.

Identifying development needs

The process of reflecting on your goals should lead you into identifying development needs. These will be skills and knowledge that you need to develop if you are to achieve your goals. Examples of development needs might include:

♦ improving your listening skills

♦ getting better at chairing meetings

♦ dealing better with interruptions

♦ learning to use a piece of software.

Deciding how you will learn

There is a very wide range of learning methods available – see, for example, Mabey and Iles (1994). These include:

♦ college or university courses – the traditional method of gaining knowledge and learning new skills

♦ off-the-job training – provided either by the company's human resource (HR) function or another training organisation

♦ on-the-job coaching – where your line manager helps you to develop a skill

♦ mentoring – where someone else in the organisation supports you

♦ learning sets or self-help learning groups – where you work in a group with colleagues to learn something

♦ self-directed learning – where you manage your own learning using other resources such as books, articles, and so on

♦ open and flexible learning – a programme of learning where you manage your own learning, but with the support of learning materials and other people.

Your choice of methods will depend on:

♦ your own preferences for ways of learning

♦ what is appropriate for the topic

♦ what is available.

Action planning

Finally:

♦ plan how you will find support – establish who will help you

♦ set deadlines – when you will complete the learning.

Now try the following activities to help you put these ideas into practice.

Activity 5
Examine your own career

Objective

Use this activity to examine your career.

As we grow and develop, so our priorities change and we spend more or less time on different activities. By imagining the future, we can gain greater control over what we are able to achieve.

Task

1   Begin by thinking about how you currently spend your time over a week. Think about how you spend your time between work, study, rest and self-care, family and friends, leisure interests and community/voluntary work. Draw a pie chart to show the proportion of your time devoted to each.

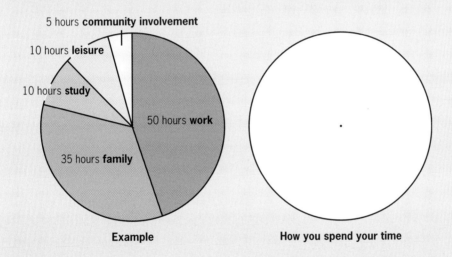

Example   **How you spend your time**

2   Now draw another pie chart showing how you spent your time ten years ago.

Ten years ago

3 Next spend a little time building a vision of the future. Sit back and relax for a moment. Think about what you would like to be doing in ten years' time. What activities would you like to be doing? Where would your priorities be?

Note down your ideas here – to capture them.

Ideas for spending time in the future:

Draw a third pie chart to show how your time would be split up in your envisioned future.

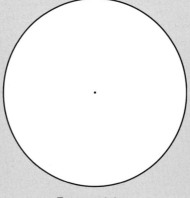

Ten years' time

Feedback

It is becoming increasingly important to reflect on your career changes, and an activity like this is one way of stimulating this reflection.

There are several things you could do to follow up this activity. For example:

1　Reflect on the changes that have happened to you over the last ten years. Which have been positive? Which have been negative? What have you achieved? What do you still want to achieve?

2　Have a go at setting some goals for the next ten years. What are the things you would need to achieve to make your vision a reality?

3　Take one of your goals and work out the main concrete steps you could take to turn this into a reality. What do you need to do and by when?

Activity 6
Plan your development

Objective

Use this activity to identify and plan ways of meeting your development needs. The activity guides you through the process.

Task

Complete the grid which follows:

1　Begin by thinking about your goals in life generally and work in particular. Ask yourself questions like:

◆　What do you enjoy doing?

◆　What do you find difficult?

◆　What would you like to be doing in five years' time?

◆　What changes do you want to make?

2　On the basis of this, identify your most important development needs. Aim for around three areas of skills and knowledge you plan to improve.

3　Next, decide which learning method you would prefer for each need.

4　Set a target deadline for reviewing progress.

5　Add any other comments such as who you might ask for help.

Personal development plan		
Relevant work goals:		
Relevant life goals:		
Development need Learning method(s)		*Target date to complete*
1		
2		
3		
Comments:		

Feedback

You will be able to use your development plan to guide you over the months, and indeed years, to come. Bear the following in mind:

◆ Your plan should be flexible – you may wish to revise it regularly as your own goals change.

◆ Your current work situation may not always be entirely in line with your plan. You will need to accept this, but keep your goals in mind nonetheless.

The importance of self-awareness

Self-awareness involves knowing and understanding yourself. It means being aware of your strengths and weaknesses, your preferences and dislikes, your ways of working with other people and your overall view of the world. It is about knowing what makes you tick.

Yvonne L'Aiguille talks about how self-awareness has been so important in her work as a nurse:

> Through the process of reflection I have the ability to recognise aspects of my behaviour that are not helpful to developing the style of nursing that I aspire to. This self-awareness, while not solving the problem, does enable me to develop a strategy for limiting its effect on my practice. It also allows me to identify particular skills that I do have, thereby increasing the likelihood that I will be able to use them more consciously in the future.

Source: *L'Aiguille* (1994)

The benefits of self-awareness

It is possible to identify three broad benefits of self-awareness for a manager.

First, knowing your personal strengths and preferences and those of the individuals in your team means that you can make the most of these in your work. It can help you to allocate and tackle tasks effectively by delegating tasks to people who are good at them and making the most of individuals with complementary and diverse strengths. Knowing where you and your team are weaker can also help you to identify areas for development and personal growth.

Second, self-awareness goes deeper than this. Knowing yourself helps you to become aware of how you see the world, and the fact that other people may have different perceptions. As Stephen Covey argues in his book *The Seven Habits of Highly Effective People*, 'self-awareness enables us to stand apart and examine even the way we "see" ourselves – our self-paradigm, the most fundamental paradigm of effectiveness'. For Covey, this influences both the way we behave and the way we see other people:

> In fact, until we take how we see ourselves (and how we see others) into account, we will be unable to understand how others see and feel about themselves and their world. Unaware, we will project our intentions on their behaviour and call

ourselves objective. This significantly limits our personal potential and our ability to relate to others as well.

Source: *Covey* (1992)

Self-awareness is therefore essential to Covey's first habit: being proactive. It is the starting point for understanding ourselves, our world and our relationships with other people.

Stephen Covey's seven habits of highly effective people

1 **Be proactive** – principles of personal vision.

2 **Begin with the end in mind** – principles of personal leadership.

3 **Put first things first** – principles of personal management.

4 **Think win/win** – principles of interpersonal leadership.

5 **Seek first to understand, then seek to be understood** – principles of empathetic communication.

6 **Synergise** – principles of creative co-operation.

7 **Sharpen the saw** – principles of balanced self-renewal.

Source: *Covey* (1992)

Third, for Daniel Goleman, self-awareness has further benefits for managers in terms of helping us deal more effectively with the difficult emotional situations that can arise at work.

Daniel Goleman: Self-awareness and emotional intelligence

For Goleman, self-awareness is the 'fundamental emotional competence'. Goleman argues that 'emotional intelligence' (EI) involves activities within five domains:

◆ knowing one's emotions

◆ managing emotions

◆ motivating oneself

◆ recognising emotions in others

◆ handling relationships.

Self-awareness is crucial to knowing one's emotions, to 'maintaining self-reflectiveness even amidst turbulent emotions'. It allows us, for example, to step back slightly from feelings of anger, observe the situation and act in a way that may help the situation to evolve positively.

Source: *Goleman* (1995)

Ways of looking at self-awareness

There are various contrasting ways of looking at self-awareness, and as a manager you may be able to draw on these. For example, some occupational psychologists suggest that there are recognisable personality differences which influence how people approach their work. Two leading writers in this field, Katherine Cook Briggs and Isabel Briggs Myers, have created a personality test known as the Myers Briggs Types Indicator (MBTI) which claims to reveal how different people realise their preferences.

Personality differences: The Myers Briggs Types Indicator

Developed from the work of Swiss psychiatrist Carl Jung (1895–1961), Myers and Briggs identified four dimensions or 'scales' of behaviour, as follows:

- **Dimension 1:** where you draw your energy from – outside yourself (extroverted) or from within (introverted)

- **Dimension 2:** how you gather information about the world – in a literal, sequential way (sensing) or in a figurative, random way (intuition)

- **Dimension 3:** the way you prefer to make decisions – objectively and impersonally (thinking) or subjectively and interpersonally (feeling)

- **Dimension 4:** to do with your day-to-day lifestyle – whether you prefer to be decisive and planned (judging) or flexible and spontaneous (perceiving).

On each of these four scales there is a range of possible preferences. For example, in the case of the second scale, some people obtain information in an imaginative (intuitive) way while others prefer a more data-driven (sensing) approach. In the case of the third scale, some people are more likely to take decisions on a rational (thinking) basis, while others will place greater emphasis on an emotional (feeling) basis.

Comparing these two scales, Myers and Briggs identified four basic conceptual types:

- intuitives with thinking
- intuitives with feeling
- sensors with thinking
- sensors with feeling.

For Myers and Briggs, the other two scales act as **modifying** factors on the basic conceptual types to give a total of sixteen different 'personality types'.

Source: *Myers Briggs* (1962)

The concept of personality preferences clearly has potential value in developing your own self-awareness, and you may like to carry out the Myers Briggs Types Indicator (or a similar instrument) if you have the opportunity.

When using personality types to develop self-awareness, it is important not to label yourself – or other people – unduly on the basis of particular typologies or the results of personality tests. For example, if a test suggests that you have a preference to take decisions on the basis of feelings, there is a potential risk of reinforcing this behaviour. In practice, you may find it is better to look for opportunities to increase your use of thinking approaches whenever this may help you to take better decisions. Myers and Briggs themselves recognise that while an individual may have their own preferences on each dimension, they may be able to use different approaches. Of course, people also develop and results may vary at different times in their lives.

An alternative approach is the personal SWOT analysis. A SWOT analysis – which you may encounter as a tool for looking at your organisation – involves identifying strengths, weaknesses, opportunities and threats.

A personal SWOT analysis

To carry out your personal SWOT analysis, you begin by looking at how things are at present:

♦ What are your **strengths**?

♦ What are your **weaknesses**?

You then go on to look at the changes in the wider environment that may have an impact on you in the future:

♦ What **opportunities** are likely to arise?

♦ What **threats** may you encounter?

As a result of a personal SWOT analysis, you can plan to make the most of your strengths and opportunities – for example, by asking to be involved in a new project. You can also take steps to reduce the impact of weaknesses and threats – for example, by developing new skills or by anticipating changes.

There is more guidance on the SWOT analysis in the activity which follows.

Activity 7
Conduct a personal SWOT analysis

Objective

Use this activity to carry out your personal SWOT analysis.

Task

To carry out your personal SWOT analysis, you begin by looking at how things are at present:

1 What are your **strengths**? These are the things that you do well in your work.

2 What are your **weaknesses**? These are the things that you find difficult in your work.

You then go on to look at the changes in the wider environment that may have an impact on you in the future.

3 What **opportunities** are likely to arise? These could be opportunities to get involved in exciting new work or projects, to work with new people, to develop new skills, and so on.

4 What **threats** may you encounter? These could be changes in the organisation that may have a negative impact on you or your team.

Strengths:	*Weaknesses:*

Opportunities:	*Threats:*

Feedback

As a result of a personal SWOT analysis you can do four things. Try to answer the following questions:

1 How can you make the most of your strengths?

2 What can you do to reduce the impact of the weaknesses you have identified? For example, which new skills could you develop?

3 How can you ensure that you seize opportunities? For example, how could you make sure you become involved in an exciting new project?

4 How can you take steps to reduce the impact of threats – for example, by developing strengths in anticipation of change?

◆ Recap

This theme has explored personal development and career planning.

◆ **Examine the impact of changing career patterns on personal development**
Changes in career patterns have implications for your personal development. Today's organisational climate demands some career planning to help set goals, identify development needs and decide how you will learn.

◆ **Consider your career path and personal objectives**
A review of your current working and leisure patterns will help you to build a vision for the future.

◆ **Plan your professional development to acquire the skills and knowledge you will require in the future**
Reflection on your goals in life should include asking questions about what you enjoy doing, what you find difficult, where you want to be in five years, what changes you want to make.

◆ **Use a range of approaches to explore your values and performance**
There are a number of ways to explore your values and performance, including using emotional intelligence and Myers Briggs tests. The personal SWOT analysis was presented as a core approach.

 **More @**

Covey, S. R. (1992) *The Seven Habits of Highly Effective People*, **Simon and Schuster**
One of the key messages of this book is that in order to perform more effectively you need a 'paradigm shift' – a change in perception and interpretation of how the world works. Covey takes you through this change, which affects how you perceive and act regarding productivity, time management, positive thinking, developing your 'proactive muscles' (acting with initiative rather than reacting) and much more.

Goleman, D. (1995) *Emotional intelligence*, **Bantam**
This book is based on brain and behavioural research. Daniel Goleman defines emotional intelligence in terms of self-awareness, altruism, personal motivation, empathy and the ability to love and be loved. People who possess high emotional intelligence are the people who truly succeed in work as well as play, building flourishing careers and lasting, meaningful relationships.

Handy, C. (1991) *The Age of Unreason*, **Random Century**
Handy recognises the way life and work are changing in this radical new look at the age. This book explores the possibilities of upside-down personal thinking, personal re-framing, telecommuting, the electronic shamrock, the inverted doughnut, horizontal fast-tracking, portfolio marriages.

Murdock, A. and Scutt, C. (2002) 3rd edition, *Personal Effectiveness*, **Butterworth-Heinemann**
Personal Effectiveness encourages managers to develop self-knowledge and apply this to their behaviour, both in relation to their own job performance and in the role of leading and managing others. Through reviewing progress within your area of managerial responsibility, you will improve your own opportunities and prospects. This book inspires managers to continuously develop and upgrade their set of skills, knowledge and behaviours to be appropriate for effective leadership in the twenty-first century.

www.personalpowernow.com.au/Articles/index.asp
Try out the **Personal power now** website for some really interesting articles on the subject of self-help, inspiration, mind power and development.

www.emotionalintelligence.co.uk/index.htm
The **Centre for Applied Emotional Intelligence** is a useful source of information about practitioners and research. It covers EI, trust, multiple intelligences and EI for a competitive edge.

www.dti.gov.uk/pwp
Partnerships with People aims to help organisations bring the best out of their people to achieve significantly enhanced business performance. The package includes a practical guide, worksheets and case studies.

Full references are provided at the end of the book.

3 Exploring perceptions and diversity

Our self-awareness is closely linked to the way we see the world – what psychologists tend to call our 'perception' of ourselves and others. Here we introduce some ideas about perception and examine ways in which you may be able to explore your self-perception and awareness.

Developing self-awareness will help you to become increasingly conscious of the differences between people. In your role as a manager you will often have to manage the differences between the people you work with if you are to build a cohesive and effective team. This theme looks at some of the sources of diversity among people and ways in which managers can recognise and embrace diversity.

This theme explores the value of different perspectives and diversity. You will:

◆ **Examine different views about perception**

◆ **Find ways to increase your self-perception**

◆ **Examine ideas of individual and cultural diversity**

◆ **Develop positive strategies for recognising and embracing diversity.**

How we see the world

It can be tempting to believe that we all see the world in which we live and work in the same way. In practice, things are more complex. The concept of perception is one that has occupied psychologists for many years. So what is perception? Kakabadse et al. define it as:

> The process by which people select, organise and interpret external sensory stimuli and information into terms and categories which are consistent with their own frames of reference and personal views of the world.

Source: *Kakabadse et al.* (1987)

An understanding of perception is an important element of the manager's toolkit. As Stephen Covey puts it:

> We must look at the lens through which we see the world, as well as the world we see – the lens itself shapes how we interpret the world.

Source: *Covey* (1992)

For Covey, 'the way we see governs the way we behave'. This view echoes the ideas of one of the leading psychologists on perception, George Kelly, who argues that our view of the world is the result of a complex blend of experience and interpretation.

George Kelly: How we construct our view of the world

The psychologist George Kelly argues that the way we see and interpret the world influences our behaviour. For Kelly, 'behaviour is an experiment' – we use our experience to create a range of 'constructs' which we use to interpret events and experiences and to predict what may happen to us.

Kelly argues that this has much in common with how scientists use theories and hypotheses as the basis for their research.

As we apply our personal constructs to new experiences, we test them out. We may encounter experiences which make us question one or more of our personal constructs, and when this happens we make changes to them. As a result our personal constructs are not set in stone; we are constantly testing our assumptions and refining or changing our constructs.

Source: *Kelly* (1970)

Recognising that our perception of the world is something we have constructed ourselves – and above all that other people have constructed very different views of the world – is a major challenge for many managers. To quote Covey again, it is important to realise that people see the world 'not as it is, but as they are'.

If we don't look closely at our perceptions, several problems may result:

◆ We may see ourselves in a very different way from how other people see us. If someone has a more positive view of themselves than others have, they may come across as arrogant. Many people go to the other extreme, however, and undervalue themselves with the consequence that they lack self-confidence.

◆ We may see other people in a very different way from how they perceive themselves. This could lead us to misinterpret their behaviour, or to act in a way that they find upsetting.

◆ We may go further and project our own perceptions onto other people. This can lead us to screen out aspects of another person that do not fit with our view of them. It may also lead to self-fulfilling prophesies – if we expect someone to act in a particular way, our own behaviour may provoke the person to behave in this way.

Examining your own perception

There is a range of techniques that you can use to examine your perception. One that is widely used in management development is the 'Johari window' which offers a model for comparing what we know about ourselves with what other people know about us.

The Johari window

The Johari window (named after the two psychologists who developed it, Joe and Harry) is a tool for exploring our self-perception. This approach provides a model for examining what we know about ourselves, and what other people know about us (see Figure 3.1).

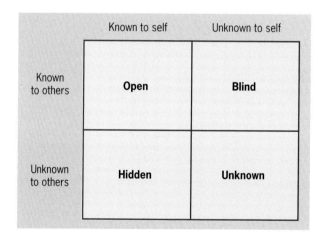

Figure 3.1 *The Johari window*   Source: *Luft and Ingham* (1955)

According to this model, our self-perception can increase in two ways:

1 **By self-disclosure**, where we tell other people things about ourselves that they did not know.

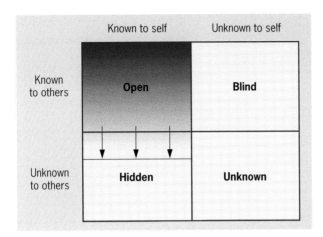

2 **By feedback**, where other people tell us things about ourselves that we did not know.

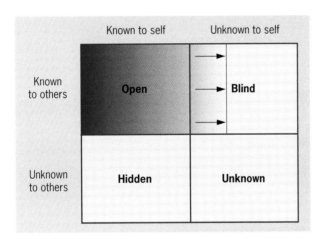

The combination of these two processes can increase the open area in the window.

Another way of looking at your perception is to examine what Stephen Covey calls your 'basic paradigms'. Covey uses the idea of personal 'centres' as a means of exploring these paradigms.

Finding your centre

Covey argues that most people have a centre which has 'all-encompassing effects' on every aspect of their lives. He describes several such centres:

◆ spouse centredness

◆ family centredness

◆ money centredness

◆ work centredness

- possession centredness
- pleasure centredness
- friend/enemy centredness
- church centredness
- self centredness.

For Covey, your centre will influence how you see all aspects of your life. If, for example, your centre is work, then you will see your partner and family as a help or hindrance to work. You may see leisure activities as a waste of time, and so on.

Source: *Covey* (1992)

Activity 8
Use the Johari window

Objective

Use this activity to:

- explore your own perceptions
- explore the perceptions that others have of you.

Task

1 Consider one work relationship that you have. Choose someone who you feel reasonably comfortable with, but where you feel there is scope to improve your relationship.

2 What could you tell the person about yourself that would expand the open area and squeeze the hidden area?

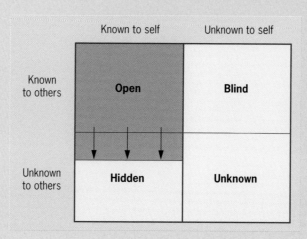

What I could disclose:

3 How might you invite feedback from the other person that might
   help move knowledge from the blind area to the open area, and so
   expand the open area again?

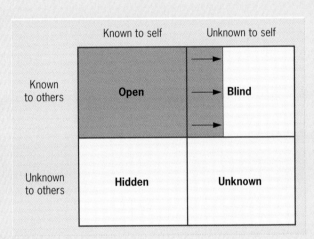

How I might invite feedback:

Valuing the differences

On an individual level, people differ enormously. Recognising these differences and why they occur helps you to understand what makes people tick, and how they can make a positive contribution in their work.

Individual diversity

This section looks at individaul diversity, cultural diversity and concludes with a review of positive strategies for accepting diversity.

People differ in many ways. Some of the key differences that a manager can probe include:

♦ **Abilities** – it can be helpful to reach shared understanding with other people of their strengths and weaknesses, and the background and experiences that underpin these. An example might be somebody's ability to work effectively within a team. It is crucial to recognise the difference between attainment, where people are now, and potential, what they would be capable of given the necessary support and encouragement.

♦ **Preferences** – just because someone is good at something does not mean that they enjoy doing it. Consider what they prefer doing – and indeed the more fundamental reasons why they work and what they want to achieve through work. An example might be whether somebody prefers working in a small team or a larger team. Again, people differ markedly in their preferences, and what satisfies one person may frustrate another.

♦ **Values** – our values underpin the way we think and behave. Kakabadse et al. (1987) define values as 'the underlying drives which influence the attitudes and behavioural patterns of individuals, groups and even organisations'. An example might be how important the team is to an individual. Our values influence how we manage, how we behave in groups, how we do our work and indeed the extent to which we believe in what we are doing.

An awareness of individual differences like this is in itself crucial. However, writers like Stephen Covey and David Goleman go a stage further. They argue that we must not just seek to understand diversity – we must also value it. As Covey puts it:

> The person who is truly effective has the humility and reverence to recognise his own perceptual limitations and appreciate the rich resources available through the hearts and minds of other human beings. That person values the differences because those differences add to his knowledge, to his understanding of reality.

Source: *Covey* (1992)

So, diversity can be extremely positive. The manager who can make the most of individual differences can really bring together the skills, knowledge and capabilities of their team.

Cultural diversity

It's not just individual diversity that managers must recognise, however. The organisations in which we work are also culturally diverse culturally in that different teams or sections may have their own cultures with different values and priorities. This also reflects the increasingly multicultural nature of the societies that many of us live in today. What is more, increased ease of mobility and growing cross-frontier trading means that more and more managers will travel abroad or work in multinational organisations with sites and customers across the world.

Cultural diversity brings a further set of challenges. People from different cultural backgrounds may look different. They may have very different religious and ethical values. They may have different customs and patterns of behaviour.

Such differences can easily lead to bias, stereotyping and out-and-out prejudice as, for example, when people from one ethnic background are less likely to gain promotion than those from another ethnic background. Daniel Goleman (1995) argues that 'prejudices are a kind of emotional learning that occurs early in life'. Such deep-seated prejudices are 'especially hard to eradicate entirely, even in people who as adults feel it is wrong to hold them'.

Goleman argues that stereotypes like these change very slowly. He claims that 'it is more practical to try to suppress the expression of bias rather than trying to eliminate the attitude itself'. He also argues that:

> To stop at battling prejudice in the workplace is to miss a greater opportunity: taking advantage of the creative and entrepreneurial possibilities that a diverse workforce can offer. A working group of varied strength and perspectives, if it can operate in harmony, is likely to come to better, more creative and more effective solutions.

Source: *Goleman* (1995)

Positive strategies for accepting diversity

A number of writers offer strategies for accepting and embracing diversity. Much thinking in this area has been influenced by the ideas of Carl Rogers, a leading figure in counselling psychology. For Rogers, we need to start by focusing on how we view other people.

Carl Rogers: Unconditional positive regard

In his book *On Becoming a Person* (1961), Carl Rogers describes the concept of unconditional positive regard. He argues that within supportive relationships it is important to value and respect the personal worth of other people. This suggests that you will be most effective as a manager if you demonstrate genuine confidence in the abilities of the people in your team to perform and to develop. Rogers suggests three key elements of this:

♦ 'realness' or 'genuineness' – being able to convey an honest and open picture of yourself as a person

♦ prizing, acceptance and trust – being able to accept and value the other person as a human being

♦ empathetic understanding – being able to see how the other person sees things, to put yourself in their shoes.

Source: *Rogers* (1961)

A practical strategy for accepting diversity comes from neuro-linguistic programming (NLP), which is outlined in O'Connor and McDermott (1996).

NLP: Second positioning

Second positioning is, in effect, an extension of the idea of 'putting yourself into someone else's shoes'. When faced with diversity or conflict, you can put yourself into two positions:

♦ The first position is your own position – it involves how you think and feel about a situation

♦ The second position involves looking at the situation from the point of view of the other person.

The move between the two positions involves a conscious step. It is also possible to adopt a third position, that of an independent observer who watches the interaction.

Source: *Derived from O'Connor and McDermott* (1996)

The ideas of Carl Rogers and second positioning focus on accepting and valuing diversity at an individual level. Diversity is also an issue for organisations, however.

Increasingly – in particular in the US – organisations are looking at ways of countering prejudice and encouraging positive attitudes towards diversity right across the organisation. Daniel Goleman argues that while one-off diversity training courses often have little effect on bias and prejudice, more thorough courses can have a real impact.

Daniel Goleman: Success in diversity training

Goleman highlights a number of ingredients of successful diversity training programmes:

◆ Change norms by taking an active stance against any acts of discrimination, from top management down

◆ Reject any intolerance – it is vital that people do not close their eyes to acts of discrimination

◆ Encourage people to speak out, even against low-key acts of discrimination or harassment

◆ Practice perspective taking (rather like second positioning) to encourage empathy and tolerance

◆ Encourage people from diverse backgrounds to work together in a team to achieve a common goal.

Source: *Goleman* (1995)

Valuing people with disabilities

◆ Avoid using disabling language, for example, 'people with disabilities' rather than 'disabled people'

◆ Consider the effects of environments and individual perceptions in planning interventions

◆ Emphasise abilities rather than limitations

◆ Accept that people with disabilities have the same rights to community participation as their non-disabled peers.

Source: *Guirdham* (1995)

The following activities further explore the topic of perceptions and diversity. The activities ask you to make a comparison of perceptions of a meeting and examine diversity through 'positioning'.

Activity 9
Compare perceptions of a meeting

Objective

Use this activity to compare perceptions of a meeting.

It is common for different people to have different perceptions of an event or experience. This may be particularly true of meetings. As one manager told us:

> I recently spoke, on separate occasions, with two colleagues who had attended the same meeting. Both commented that the other person had spoken too much during the meeting and had caused it to run on too long. Both seemed unaware that they may have spoken too much themselves.

Task

1   Select a meeting that you will need to attend over the next week or so. Plan to record your perceptions of the meeting.

2   Ask two colleagues who will attend the meeting if they will do the same. You could make them a copy of the record sheet provided here. Arrange to discuss the meeting individually with them afterwards.

3   When the meeting has finished, note your perceptions in the record sheet.

4   After the meeting, debrief the other people in turn. Make notes of what they say.

5   Examine what each person said and reflect on findings.

How well it went:

What went well and what went less well:

How well you think you contributed to the meeting:

How well others contributed:

How the meeting might have been improved:

Activity 10
Explore diversity

Objective

Use this activity to explore diversity through 'positioning'.

'Second positioning' involves looking at an event or experience from three different positions.

The move between the positions involves a conscious step – you need to deliberately picture yourself stepping into someone else's shoes.

Task

Select a recent event or experience at work where you have been conscious of difficulties in a relationship you have with a colleague. Reflect on this experience from three different points of view:

1 Begin by adopting the first position. What was your own experience of the situation? How did you think and feel about it? Note down your thoughts and feelings.

2 Then adopt the second position. Picture yourself as the other person and try to look at the experience as they might have seen it. What do you think the experience was like from their point of view? How might they have felt about it? Again, note down your thoughts and feelings.

3 Then adopt the third position. Picture yourself as an independent observer watching the interaction from outside. What might they have thought about the situation? Again, note down your thoughts and feelings.

Finally, reflect on what you have learnt about the event and about the other person's experience of it.

First position: thoughts and feelings

Second position: thoughts and feelings

Third position: thoughts and feelings

Feedback

Thinking through an experience in this way should make you a little more aware of the diversity of values and behaviours that we encounter at work. You should have become more conscious of:

◆ how other people may see you – and that this perception may be different from your own

◆ why the other person may have behaved the way they did

◆ the fact that the other person's motives, hopes and fears may have been markedly different from your own.

There may be things you can do immediately as a result of this – you may for example identify an action you could take that might have a positive impact on your relationship.

There may also be understanding that you can take into other areas of your work.

◆ Recap

Examine different views about perception
One of the key perspectives on perception is the Johari window which supports self-knowledge through increasing self-disclosure and feedback from others.

Find ways to increase your self-perception
There are a number of ways suggested to help you disclose more about yourself and invite feedback, such as 'second positioning' and recognition of the value of diversity.

Examine ideas of individual and cultural diversity
An awareness of individual differences, and furthermore, that those differences present opportunities, is crucial. Different cultural values and practices not only add variety but also present positive strategic advantages.

Develop positive strategies for recognising and embracing diversity
The strategies explored include unconditional positive regard, second positioning, diversity training and valuing people with disabilities.

▶▶ More @

Kakabadse, A. and Vinnicombe, S. (2003) *Working in Organisations*, Gower
As society changes, so must its organisations; as organisations change, so must their management competencies. One of the aspects covered by this book is the new psychological contract, highlighting reliance on self whilst maintaining sensitivity to diversity concerns and discussing how power and politics can be moulded to positive advantage.

Kirton, G. and Greene, A. M. (2004) 2nd edition, *The Dynamics of Managing Diversity*, Butterworth-Heinemann
This text takes the view that the study of equality needs to consider not only issues of discrimination, but also the needs of people in relation to their diverse cultures and identities. It therefore takes a different approach to the issues of quality and diversity in the world of employment. *The Dynamics of Managing Diversity* discusses diversity as recognition of the differences and similarities between and among social groups, and how resulting policies must reflect these.

Rogers, C. R. (1961) *On Becoming a Person*, **Constable**
This is a classic text in the realms of psychotherapy. The author argues that in any personal relations, be it with patients, pupils, colleagues, friends or partners, the route to personal growth (for all sides) requires empathy, acceptance and truthfulness. It is an important text that people still use to direct their thinking about self-awareness and perceptions.

www.cipd.co.uk/default.cipd
The **Chartered Institute of Personnel and Development** is well worth exploring for topics such as diversity, and learning and development. There are a range of articles from *People Management* and publications. To access some of these you will need to be a member.

www.managers.org.uk/institute/home_3.asp
The **Chartered Institute of Management** website offers a range of articles and research on development topics. To access some of these you will need to be a member.

Full references are provided at the end of the book.

4   Time management

Many managers feel overwhelmed by the demands on their time.
They would like to feel more in control, and more confident of
getting through their work. This theme introduces things to
consider when starting to think about improving the way you
manage your time.

You will consider how to use your time **effectively** by focusing your
attention on those tasks that contribute to your goals. The first step
is to define your goals and commit yourself to them. You can then
use a framework against which you can identify priorities and
decide which tasks to delegate and which tasks should not be done
at all.

An important aspect of managing time is to use your time
efficiently. One way is to recover the time lost through
procrastination and perfectionism. Another way of increasing
your efficiency is to adopt some sound daily habits like making
good use of your prime time. A third way, close to the heart of many
managers, is to be able to speed up activities such as reading.

Finally we look at ways of planning your time, including long-term
planning of routine tasks and projects as well as planning the
coming week or day.

This theme offers techniques and ideas to support your time
management. You will:

- **Identify the benefits you would like to achieve by managing your time**
- **Define and prioritise your work objectives/goals**
- **Use planning to support you in achieving your objectives.**

Approaches to managing your time

Most managers would like to have more time to finish the day's
work, to catch up, to be on top of things, to do their job better, to
think and to spend time with their family.

Managing your time more effectively and efficiently can help you
move towards these goals. Here are some of the many potential
benefits of managing your time better:

- less time firefighting/dealing with crises

- less work to take home

- less anxiety and stress

- a sharper focus on the things that matter in terms of producing results

- more time for long-term activities, for example career planning, reading, communicating, relaxing, thinking

- better able to see your way through complex problems and challenges

- more energy.

Source: *Garratt* (1985), *Haynes* (1988), *Caunt* (2000)

This list is by no means exhaustive; you can probably think of further benefits of managing your own time better.

Barriers

When the benefits of managing time efficiently and effectively are so enticing, why do so many managers continue to have difficulty? Bliss (1991) identifies a range of barriers, including:

- Fear – for example, fear of failure, embarrassment, rejection.

- Indecision – feeling unable to make a decision. Stacks of paper sitting on the desk for a while usually reflect a pile of unmade decisions.

- Mental blocks – you keep trying to get a job done and nothing happens. Blocks can be caused by lack of facts, lack of conviction, lack of a starting point, tunnel vision, fatigue and not feeling like wanting to do the job.

- Parkinson's law – the work expands to fit the time available.

- Perfectionism – wanting to do every task perfectly uses up too much time. There is a difference between striving for excellence and striving for perfection.

- Procrastination – putting tasks off. This is a very common barrier, and linked to laziness and mental blocks.

- Being a workaholic – addicted to work. Symptoms include not taking holidays, the inability to put work out of your mind at home, a bulging briefcase, etc.

The various tools of time management can help you tackle these barriers. The first and most important step is to become aware of the barriers, then you will be in a position to make some changes.

Tools and approaches

Guidance on managing time is largely based on self-awareness, common sense and practical experience rather than any academic theory. There is no right way to manage time, rather a diverse set of tools and approaches. It is up to individuals to choose whatever is most appropriate to their style and circumstances. The three most commonly quoted time-management tools are:

◆ setting goals and objectives

◆ making plans to achieve those goals

◆ prioritising the tasks in hand.

There is also an abundance of guidance on a diverse range of time-management topics from managing interruptions and meetings to dealing more efficiently with paperwork and learning to say 'no'. Much of this guidance is in the form of self-explanatory checklists in the proliferation of books available on this topic. Other tools involve exploring and changing attitudes, for example, to deal with perfectionism and procrastination.

Working effectively 'doing the right thing'	Working efficiently 'doing things right'	Planning
Setting life goals	Overcoming procrastination	Long-term plans
Setting/identifying work goals	Overcoming perfectionism	Short-term plans
Setting objectives	Using prime time	Weekly plan
Prioritising tasks	Reading efficiently	Daily plan
Delegating	Managing the phone	To-do list
Saying 'no'	Managing interruptions	Daily habits
Analysing current use of time	Managing paperwork	
	Managing e-mails	
	Managing meetings	
	Using technology	
	Using travel and waiting time	
	Using a clear-desk approach	
	Operating an open/closed door policy	

Table 4.1 *Common tools for managing time*

While the list of time-management tools may seem daunting, bear in mind that one small change can have a dramatic effect. For the author, the simple change of working on a clear desk immediately increased her productivity by breaking the habit of looking through different piles of work without progressing any of them.

With so many tools available, it is not surprising that time-management experts have developed a variety of approaches to managing time. See the contrasting approaches of Austin and Haynes summarised here.

Austin: Spirit of time management

- Encourage an awareness of time – its nature, its cost, its value

- Clarify time problems caused by others, challenge them and modify them where possible

- Identify time problems caused by yourself, confront them and do something about them

- Adopt a positive attitude to your relationship with time, and develop good time-conscious habits

- Aim to master a relaxed method for handling time pressures without frustration or stress and for living a full life with a healthy balance between high achievement and earned relaxation.

Source: *Adapted from Austin* (1986)

Haynes: Time management in a nutshell

- Identify the portion of time you can control. Develop procedures for repetitive operations, and concentrate on high pay-off activities.

- Make best use of your personal energy cycle. Try to arrange a quiet period to match your prime time and use it for work requiring concentration.

- Establish quarterly objectives and construct plans to accomplish them. Be flexible to cope with the unexpected. Prioritise the action required to achieve objectives.

- Record your use of time using a time log, and analyse using the tests of necessity, appropriateness and efficiency.

Source: *Adapted from Haynes* (1988)

There are only three ways to make better use of your time:

1 Discontinue low-priority tasks or activities.

2 Find someone else to take some of your work.

3 Be more efficient at what you do.

Source: *Covey* (1992)

Covey identifies three generations of time management to date: starting with notes and checklists, then moving through calendars and diaries to the current state of goals, priorities and daily plans. He suggests a fourth generation is starting to move 'from a focus on things and time to enhancing relationships and achieving results'. This reflects some dissatisfaction with the impersonal aspects of efficiency and the need to integrate the human dimension into managing our time.

A different approach

> Forster is a life coach who evolved his own approach to time management having found that the conventional approaches of goal setting, prioritising, etc. had distinct limitations.
>
> > ...we cannot manage time. Time produces exactly twenty-four hours each day whether we like it or not. But it is up to us whether we fill that time with trivia or with worthwhile activities. It is not time we need to manage but ourselves – and particularly we need to learn to manage how and where we focus our attention.
>
> His techniques include:
>
> ◆ Number one tool – say 'no'. Reduce your commitments until you can give everything the attention it needs.
>
> ◆ Give tasks sufficient, regular, focused attention.
>
> ◆ Use the resistance principle – tackle the task that you are resisting most.
>
> Forster suggests that good time managers are: decisive, work from the big picture, have good systems, keep work and play in balance, are relatively unstressed, keep their attention focused, respond to fear with action.

Source: *Adapted from Forster* (2000)

Developing the strength to make changes

Hopefully this section has given some ideas and motivation for improving the way you manage your time. Bliss (1991) points out that time management is mainly common sense, but it is not widely practised because we **enjoy** being driven by events, crises, firefighting.

Forster (2000) suggests a method of overcoming this kind of barrier through 'mental strength training'. Each evening, decide on one thing you are going to do the next day without fail. This might be to put away one pile of clutter from the desk, to write one work objective or to ring a colleague to say you can devote two hours a week to their project. Be sure you are confident about carrying out the task. The following day, do it! If you succeed in carrying out the task, set a slightly more difficult task for the next day. If you fail to carry out the task, set a slightly easier task for the next day, for example, put away one item from your desk. In this way you gradually develop your mental strength in carrying out the tasks you set yourself. You can then move on to more challenging aspects of managing your time.

Analysing your use of time

A useful starting point for some people is to analyse how they currently use their time using a time log. Aspects you might want to investigate include:

◆ time spent on specific projects/tasks

◆ time spent on particular activities, for example, reading/e-mail/phone

◆ time when you are in control (proactive time) and time when you have to respond to others (reactive time)

◆ how realistically you estimate your time

◆ where the distractions come from

◆ your productive times of day.

Activity 11
The benefits of time management

Objective

Use this activity to identify the benefits you would like to achieve by managing your time better.

Task

1 Look through the list of potential benefits below, and tick those you would like to achieve.

2 Add any further benefits you can think of for yourself.

3 Write in any comments you have about the benefits you would like to gain, making them more specific to you.

Benefit	Comments
☐ Less time firefighting – dealing with crises	
☐ Less work to take home	
☐ Less anxiety and stress	
☐ Sharper focus on the things that matter in terms of producing results	
☐ More time for long-term activities, e.g. career planning, reading, communicating, relaxing, thinking	

Benefit	Comments
☐ The ability to see your way through complex problems and challenges	
☐ Enhanced reputation for competence	
☐ Greater sense of achievement	
☐ Setting a good example so your staff use their time better	
☐ More energy	
☐ More time for family and leisure	
☐ Others, write in:	

Feedback

Keeping your list of benefits in mind should help you stay motivated when you get into the hard work of making changes in the way you manage your time. You may find it helpful to discuss the benefits you aim to achieve with a colleague or friend.

Activity 12
Identify aspects of time management

Objective

Use this activity to identify aspects of time management you need to work on.

There is a wide range of tools and approaches to select from to make more effective and more efficient use of your time. Now use this activity to help you decide which tools will be helpful to you.

We suggest that you return to this activity when you have completed this theme to see if any other tools would be useful to support your time management.

Task

1   Read each of the paired statements that follow, and decide where you fit between the extremes described in the statements. Mark how well you are using the tool with an X on the dotted line in the middle column.

Example a	Example b	Example c
An X at this position would show you are using the tool well	An X at this position would show you are not using the tool at all	An X at this position would show you are using the tool to some extent
◄··X···················►	◄···················X··►	◄·········X·········►

Using this tool well	Tool and approach	Not using this tool at all
I can say right now what my work goals are	Setting goals ◄···················►	I don't know what my work goals are. I'm not sure which tasks are important and which aren't
I know which tasks are important, and which aren't, and I have a good method for deciding which tasks to tackle first	Prioritising tasks ◄···················►	I frequently don't know what to do first
I identify appropriate work to pass on to my team, and feel comfortable doing this	Delegating work ◄···················►	I can't find work to pass on/don't like passing on tasks to my team
I feel at ease saying 'no' to some tasks	Saying 'no' to tasks ◄···················►	I really don't like to say 'no' to requests, even when they're not really my job
I know roughly how much of my time I spend on each of my work areas, meetings, interruptions etc.	Logging/analysing use of time ◄···················►	I have no idea how much of my time I spend on each of my work areas, meetings, interruptions etc.
On the whole I'm good at getting on with work. I have ways of getting into the task if I find myself putting it off	Procrastination ◄···················►	I often find myself putting off tasks
I know that it's OK for work to be 'good enough'. I can recognise when I'm starting to spend too much time on a job to make it perfect	Perfectionism ◄···················►	I want to do each task as well as I possibly can, even if that means it takes a long time
I know at which times of the day I concentrate best	Using prime time ◄···················►	I've no idea at which times of day I concentrate best
I use methods to minimise the time interruptions take and to control the timing of some interruptions	Managing interruptions/ the phone ◄···················►	I am continually interrupted by other people, the phone, e-mails
I can rapidly absorb the essence of a report	Reading efficiently ◄···················►	It takes me ages to absorb the contents of a report
I can produce a short report quickly	Writing efficiently ◄···················►	It takes me ages to write a report
I have methods for keeping paperwork under control	Managing paperwork ◄···················►	Paperwork gets on top of me

I run meetings in the minimum time needed to achieve their purpose	**Managing meetings** ◄·····················►	The meetings I chair tend to run on
I plan what I will do with my travel and waiting time (even if this is relaxation)	**Using titbits of time** ◄·····················►	I usually end up wasting travel and waiting time
I prepare plans for my main tasks for the coming three/six months	**Long term planning** ◄·····················►	I keep working through the tasks and hope I'll get things done in time
I prepare a weekly/daily plan and hope I'll get things	**Weekly/daily planning** ◄·····················►	I keep working through the tasks done in time
I have some daily habits to make efficient use of my time	**Daily habits** ◄·····················►	I don't really have any daily habits that enable me to make efficient use of my time

2 Reflect on your ratings.

Which tools are you using well? It makes sense to keep using them.

Which tools are you not using that might be helpful to you? Remember that while some tools help some people, they may be totally inappropriate to you or your situation. On the other hand, try not to shirk away from a tool you really know you should use, but don't want to tackle.

3 Note down three tools you feel will most help you to manage your time better in the box below. Decide on the action you will take for each. This might include finding out more about the tool.

Tools I will use: *Action:*

1

2

3

Feedback

A single change that addresses a weak point in the way you manage your time can have a dramatic effect.

As you put it into practice you will probably become more aware of the way you are managing your time, and naturally move on to other improvements.

Effective use of time: Doing the right things

Effective use of time (doing the right things) means focusing most of your time on those tasks which contribute to your goals. The key is first to define and commit yourself to your goals, and then minimise the amount of time spent on tasks which do not contribute to your goals.

Efficient use of time (doing things right) means working through tasks at a reasonable rate. This can be achieved through techniques such as managing interruptions, overcoming procrastination, speed reading, etc. We will look at efficient use of time in the next section.

Goals

Most time experts identify having goals as a key aspect of managing time. Goals are essential to provide direction for the way you use your time in all aspects of your life. Not having goals invites the danger of frittering away time on trivial or unimportant tasks, and denies the satisfaction of achievement.

The first step is to write your goals, or in some cases to identify goals which may have already been defined for you at work.

The second step is to commit yourself wholeheartedly to your goals so it becomes second nature to focus on tasks that contribute to these goals. Without this commitment, goals will not work for you, for as Covey (1992) says:

The way you spend your time is a result of the way you see your time and the way you really see your priorities.

Source: *Covey* (1992)

Life and career goals

Having goals to provide direction to your time does not only apply to work; it is equally important for the rest of your life. Increasingly, experts recommend starting by writing 'lifetime goals' to cover the various areas of your life including, for example, family, interests, community contribution, etc.

Recognising that the traditional idea of one job for life is disappearing, Hindle (1998) recommends making career goals in both the short and long term, as shown in Figure 4.1.

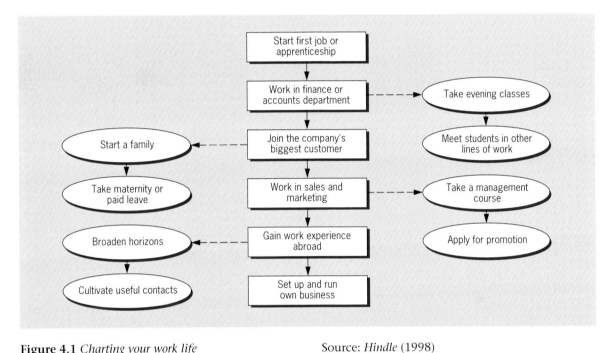

Figure 4.1 *Charting your work life*   Source: *Hindle* (1998)

Defining work goals and objectives

Most managers do not have the luxury of defining their own work goals; it is more a case of uncovering them from various business documents. Goals should form a hierarchy with the organisation's mission statement at the top, and goals/objectives from the various levels all feeding upwards into the next level, as shown in Figure 4.2.

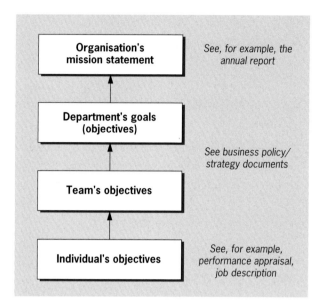

Figure 4.2 *Hierarchy of business goals*

Working down the hierarchy, the goals/objectives become more and more specific until they come to the level of the individual employee, where they are usually expressed as objectives. Ideally, objectives are developed by mutual agreement between the individual and their manager, and reviewed periodically so they can be updated to reflect changing circumstances.

Objectives should be:

◆ Specific

◆ Measurable

◆ Attainable

◆ Realistic

◆ Time specific.

Objectives that meet these criteria are often referred to as SMART. The following are examples of SMART objectives:

◆ Set up a new area team to cover Ireland by December

◆ Launch the new magazine in December

◆ Decrease customer complaints by 10 per cent this year.

Priorities

A frequent challenge to managers is which of the many jobs they are faced with should they tackle first. There are two main approaches to prioritising tasks: the ABC list and the importance versus urgency grid. In both cases, the starting point is a list of tasks to be carried out. This could be your to-do list for the week or the day.

ABC

- ◆ **Priority A – must do.** These are critical tasks which must be carried out.

- ◆ **Priority B – should do.** These tasks will contribute to performance, but are not essential or do not have critical deadlines.

- ◆ **Priority C – nice to do.** These tasks contribute little or nothing to goals, and can be eliminated or postponed. However, we are often drawn to them because they can be interesting or fun activities.

Importance v urgency

The importance–urgency grid refines the process of prioritising tasks by making the assessment of importance and urgency more explicit. The procedure is to write each item from your to-do list into one of the four quadrants of the grid shown in Figure 4.3.

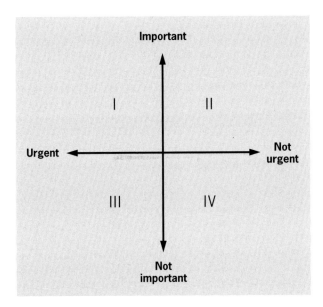

Figure 4.3 *Importance–urgency grid*   Source: *Adapted from Covey* (1992)

Covey identifies the following types of activity which typically fall into each quadrant (see also Figure 4.4).

> **Quadrant I – urgent and important**
> For activities in this quadrant the urgency usually takes over and we react by tackling the task. However, since the task is important, there is a danger that in dealing with it in a reactive, urgent way, it may not be given enough time. Working in quadrant I is stressful, so it may be necessary to seek relief in the easier and more pleasant activities of quadrant IV.
>
> **Quadrant II – important but not urgent**
> This is the quadrant in which effective time managers spend most time. It involves focusing your time on tasks which are

important, but because they are not urgent you are able to devote sufficient attention to them.

Quadrant III – urgent but not important

Spending a lot of time on urgent but not important matters probably means you are spending too much time reacting to other people's demands. Like quadrant I activities, this can be stressful. Tasks in this quadrant warrant little, if any, attention.

Quadrant IV – not important and not urgent

This is the escape route when the going gets tough, a comfortable place to be but entirely unproductive in terms of achieving goals.

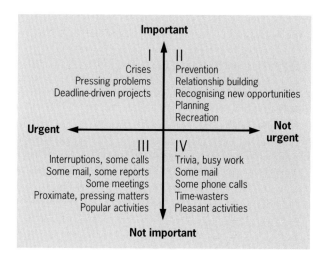

Figure 4.4 *Types of activity in the importance–urgency grid*

To use your time effectively means:

♦ spending most of your time in quadrant II

♦ keeping quadrant I under control by spending more time in quadrant II

♦ staying out of quadrants III and IV because the work is not important.

Covey's focus on quadrant II

Quadrant II is the heart of personal management. It deals with things that are not urgent, but are important...like building relationships, writing a personal mission statement, long-range planning, preparation – all those things we know we need to do, but somehow seldom get around to doing because they aren't urgent.

Results of giving attention to quadrant II:

♦ vision, perspective

♦ balance

◆ discipline

◆ control

◆ few crises.

In this approach, the key question to ask is 'What is the most important thing I should do now?' Important tasks are those which lead to goals. You must have a commitment to these goals.

Source: *Covey* (1992)

Tasks you should not do

It should be clear from the importance–urgency grid that some tasks which find their way onto our to-do lists should not be tackled at all. There are three ways of dealing with such tasks: delegation, saying 'no' and no action.

What should you delegate?

As a manager, you may have subordinates to whom you can pass on some routine tasks. Fleming (1997) identifies the types of tasks to delegate:

◆ routine tasks

◆ tasks which others could do better/more cheaply.

What should you say 'no' to?

It is not appropriate for you to do some of the tasks that arrive on your desk because they do not contribute to your goals. While everyone spends some time on such tasks, they should be kept to a minimum. They could come from your manager, your colleagues, your customers or your suppliers.

Saying 'no'

Mark Forster (2000) promotes 'saying no' as the most important time-management tool because it enables you to give sufficient attention to your important tasks. He gives the following tips:

◆ Be prepared to repeat your 'no' at least once.

◆ Say something like, 'I appreciate you asking me, but I can't fit that into my priorities at the moment.'

◆ If it is your boss asking you to do something, try saying, 'I can't fit that into my work priorities at the moment. Is there something you'd like me to put on hold so I can fit this in?'

The activities which follow will help you to write your goals and prioritise your tasks.

Activity 13
Write your goals

Objective

This activity will help you to define or find your work goals/objectives.

Having a set of well-defined goals is crucial to managing yourself at work. Goals, which are often split into more detailed objectives, define what you aim to achieve. They help you identify the important tasks you should spend most time on.

Goals/objectives should be:

◆ Specific

◆ Measurable

◆ Attainable

◆ Realistic

◆ Time specific.

Task

Scan through the list of tasks below, and select the one which is most appropriate for your situation.

If you do not know your job goals/objectives:

1 See if you can find them in your job appraisal form from last year, or in the strategy document for your department. Then move on to task three.

2 If there are no work goals/objectives:

◆ make a list of your main areas of work

◆ draft some goals/objectives for each area of work

◆ arrange to talk them through with your manager.

If you already have work goals/objectives:

3 Review them to see how comprehensive, realistic and up to date they are. Arrange to discuss them with your manager if you feel they need to be updated.

4 Write the objectives for a project you run or are involved in. Discuss them with the members of your project team.

5 Write your career goals, using the example in the previous section, **Effective use of time: doing the right things**, as a prompt.

Goals/objectives:

Feedback

Now that you have written down some goals, the next step is to commit yourself to them so they become embedded in your thinking and direct your activities. If you feel there are some goals to which you cannot commit yourself, you should reconsider them.

Activity 14
Prioritise your tasks

Objective

Use this activity to:

◆ prioritise your 'to do' list

◆ identify tasks you do not need to do.

Prioritising tasks a day or week in advance helps you plan your day's work. This activity asks you to use the importance–urgency grid to prioritise your 'to do' list.

Task

1 If you don't already have one, make a list of tasks to do today or this week.

2 Plot the tasks on the grid provided here according to their importance and urgency.

3 Review all important tasks to see if some of them are suitable for delegation.

4 Review all non-important tasks to see which ones you can drop.

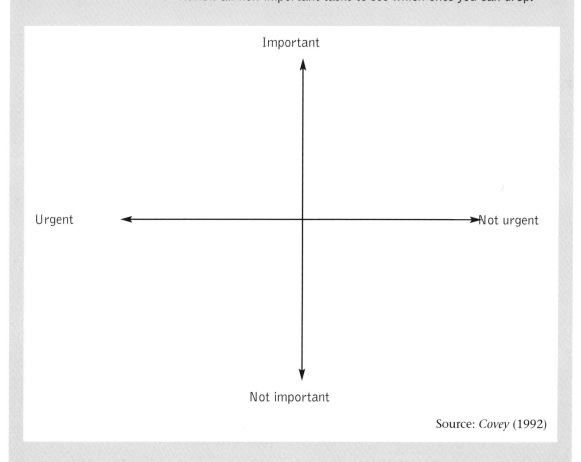

Source: *Covey* (1992)

Tasks I could delegate:

Tasks I should drop:

Feedback

Ideally, a large proportion of your tasks are important but not urgent (quadrant II) in the tasks diagram. This means you can plan to give them the time they deserve. If you have a lot of tasks that are important and urgent (quadrant I), you are probably being driven by crises and deadlines. If you have many tasks that are not important (quadrants III and IV), you should focus more attention on the tasks that contribute to your goals.

Efficient use of time: Doing things right

The first aspect of using time efficiently is to check whether your attitudes are causing you to waste time. Habitual procrastination and perfectionism are common time-wasters which can, with some effort, be beaten.

Beating procrastination

The following tips for beating procrastination are adapted from Caunt (2000) and Fleming (1997).

Recognise excuses:

- I haven't got all the information yet
- I don't have time right now to do it justice
- Other deadlines are more pressing
- If I don't do anything it may go away.

Identify underlying reasons:

♦ fear of failure or of making a mistake

♦ boredom

♦ uncertainty of how to tackle the task

♦ perfectionism – unwilling to start unless it can be done perfectly.

Adopt strategies:

♦ Recognise you have a problem, and identify the real reason

♦ Give difficult tasks a high priority

♦ Schedule time in your diary for tasks you do not like

♦ Do something (anything!) to make a start

♦ Divide large jobs up into small chunks, and do a little each day

♦ Note that tasks you avoid often turn out to be less fearsome than expected.

Perfectionism

There is a difference between striving for excellence and striving for perfection. The first is attainable, gratifying and healthy. The second is unattainable, frustrating and neurotic. It's also a terrible waste of time.

Source: *Bliss* (1991)

Bliss gives inventory taking as an example where all major items must be accounted for, while a system of 'sensible approximation' for minor items may be quite adequate.

Tips for beating perfectionism

♦ Identify why you are a perfectionist:

  – lacking confidence, so unwilling to complete the job

  – getting bogged down in the details of the task

  – unable to give up the job until it is perfect

♦ Recognise and apply Pareto's law: for a task, 80 per cent of results are achieved through 20 per cent of effort; conversely, 80 per cent of effort only produces 20 per cent of results

♦ Recognise that it is a better use of time for results to be 'good enough' rather than perfect.

Source: *Caunt* (2000) and *Bliss* (1991)

Beating procrastination and perfectionism takes real effort, but will pay dividends in time saved in the long run.

Use daily habits

The second aspect of using your time efficiently is to review your daily habits. Depending on your circumstances, your way of working and your personal preferences, some will be more appropriate to you than others.

Capitalise on your prime time

'Larks' are people with high energy early in the morning, whereas 'owls' have high energy late at night. Each person has their personal energy cycle, and it pays to become aware of your 'highs' and 'lows'.

If you don't already know the pattern of your energy cycle (see Figure 4.5), you can discover it by observing the times of day when you feel energised and those when you feel more lethargic. If you find this difficult, try asking your family, friends or colleagues.

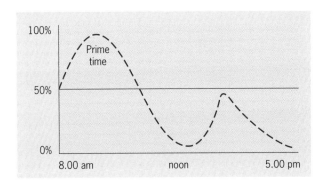

Figure 4.5 *Typical energy cycle*   Source: *Haynes* (1988)

Once you know your energy cycle, which may be quite different from the example, you can use it to schedule tasks requiring high concentration into your prime time and routine tasks into the troughs. Bliss (1991) suggests that the first two hours of the day are prime time for many people, yet their time is often taken up with routine tasks, such as the mail, phone calls, etc., whereas this time should be devoted to important tasks which contribute to their goals.

Adair (1988) suggests that many people have most energy in the hour or so before breakfast, which can be a time of solitude and silence. If you make use of this time, be sure to compensate with time off during the 'working' day.

Manage distractions and interruptions

Distractions and interruptions are a major threat to using time efficiently because they break concentration, and it is often difficult to get started again. While some interruptions are inevitable, there are steps you can take to reduce them or manage them so they are less intrusive.

Avoid distracting yourself

- ◆ Keep a clear desk to avoid distracting yourself when the going gets tough

- ◆ Have a prioritised to-do list.

Manage interruptions

- ◆ Make it known which times of the day you welcome/do not welcome interruptions

- ◆ Arrange a swap where you and a colleague take calls for each other when you need to concentrate

- ◆ When interrupted, ask yourself which is more important: the interruption or the task you are working on

- ◆ Be prepared to tactfully say 'no' to 'Have you got a minute?'

- ◆ Keep the interruption short

- ◆ Be human – ruthless but gracious.

Manage phone calls

- ◆ Plan what you have to say with short notes – this helps avoid a rambling conversation which is time-consuming

- ◆ Batch your calls, for example before lunch or towards the end of the day

- ◆ Time your calls with an egg-timer, and aim to complete each within three minutes.

Source: *Derived from Fleming* (1997), *Bliss* (1991), *Adair* (1988)

When faced with long lists of tips like this, it is important to identify the one you think will have most effect and try it out.

To-do lists

Having a list of tasks to do for the day or the week, with priorities clearly marked, avoids wasting time thinking about what you are going to do next. It is good practice to review your list at the end of the day, and to make up your list for the next day. This means the next morning you can get started straightaway on the important tasks.

Slots of time

All managers find themselves with slots of dead time, for example, when commuting or travelling, or waiting for a customer who has been delayed or for a meeting to start. One approach to these slots of time is to use them for quiet reflection as an antidote to the pressures of the day. Another approach is to use this time to complete routine tasks such as filling in your travel claim form.

> **Tips for using slots of time**
>
> ◆ Always have some small, routine tasks with you
>
> ◆ Prepare a 'travel kit', particularly if you are a regular traveller, for example laptop, mobile phone, highlighter, pocket recorder, note cards, notebook.

Speed up your activities

The third aspect of using your time efficiently is to find ways to speed up the task in hand. Some of the tips already mentioned, such as splitting the task into manageable chunks, are relevant here.

Reading and writing

Most managers feel they have more paperwork than they can cope with. With practice, it is possible to dramatically cut down the amount of time spent reading and yet absorb more. Being organised cuts down the time required to write reports.

> **Tips for efficient reading**
>
> ◆ Get an idea of the structure through the contents/headings/summary
>
> ◆ Move to the part of the document which is relevant to you
>
> ◆ Learn to skim read – the essence of a paragraph is usually contained in the first and last sentence – practise highlighting key words
>
> ◆ Aim to get the feel of a document rather than reading every word
>
> ◆ Prepare a mind map of the key points – keep it with the document so you can quickly recall the content.
>
> **Tips for efficient writing**
>
> ◆ Write down your objective(s) for the document
>
> ◆ Prepare a series of headings to meet the objectives (look for ideas from similar documents)
>
> ◆ Only write things which contribute to your objectives
>
> ◆ Start writing anywhere in the document to get going – this is easy with word-processing packages
>
> ◆ For a long document, plan to write a section a day.

Using technology

Technology is a double-edged sword for efficient use of time. On the one hand, e-mail, the Internet and software packages are great time savers because they help us carry out tasks very quickly. On the other hand, it is easy to get absorbed by, for example, an Internet search and end up wasting time.

73

Plan your time

> The first rule of planning is that you can't plan and work at the same time.

Source: *Bliss* (1991)

A few minutes spent planning a task can save time in the long run. When managers are busy, they may feel there is no time to plan, and end up getting involved in the task before planning it out. If possible, leave a gap between the planning and execution of a task; for example, plan your day the afternoon before or plan your project well before the start date. That way you can plan with more objectivity than if you are about to launch into the task.

Estimating the time required

Estimating the time a task will take is a core aspect of planning your time.

There are two aspects to estimating the time required for a task:

◆ The **actual time** that will be spent wholly on the task.
  If half an hour is slotted into the diary to prepare the headings for a report, you will be very frustrated if it ends up taking hours.

◆ The **elapsed time** needed for the task to be completed. You might estimate it will take four weeks for the report to be drafted by you, checked by your boss and approved by the project group.

Fleming (1997) suggests the time needed to carry out a task is difficult to get right because:

◆ we may not know how long the task will take until we get into it

◆ there are likely to be interruptions

◆ others, whom we rely on to get the task done, may let us down.

So:

◆ base your estimates on experience

◆ anticipate likely problems and hold-ups.

Long-term plans

Planning in the long term takes two forms: planning routine activities and planning one-off projects.

Planning routine tasks

Most organisations have routine activities which take place year in, year out. A wall planner is a good way to display key events such as budget reviews, sales conferences, business trips, recruitment drive, staff appraisal. The tasks involved can then be added to the wall planner (see Table 4.2).

Steps to schedule routine work	Example
Identify key event(s)	Sales conference
List the activities involved:	
– preparation activities	Production of leaflets
– activities during the event	Three days on the stand
– follow-up activities	Pass sales leads on to Sue
	Hold review meeting
Estimate the time involved	Four days
Schedule each activity	Mark on wall planner

Table 4.2 *Planning routine activities*

Estimating the time required for routine activities should be fairly accurate provided the time taken in the past has been monitored.

Planning a long-term project

Any non-routine task which is going to take more than a couple of weeks needs to be planned in advance to ensure the appropriate activities are identified and scheduled and that the deadline will be met. The following list summarises the steps involved.

Steps to develop a long-term plan:

◆ Set objectives

◆ Identify the tasks required to achieve the objectives

◆ Break large tasks down into sub-tasks

◆ Estimate the time required for each task, allowing for contingencies

◆ Schedule the activities, taking account of:
  – any final deadline
  – any dependencies, for example, task A has to be completed before task B can start

◆ Use appropriate planning aids:
  – wall charts to show main activities and milestones
  – project-planning software.

Estimating the time for one-off projects is difficult if there is no similar experience to use as a basis. It is therefore very important to slot in some contingency time for unexpected delays.

Weekly and daily plans

When it comes to planning the week or day, you usually find yourself planning how to get through a list of tasks which has been generated from your long-term plans.

Tips for planning your day

♦ Make a to-do list the day before

♦ Break any large tasks down into manageable chunks

♦ Prioritise the list (using ABC or importance v urgency)

♦ Schedule fixed events in your diary or organiser

♦ Schedule any routine activities into your diary, for example, half an hour for phone calls after lunch

♦ Identify any tasks which depend on completion of another task

♦ Schedule chunks of time for important tasks into your diary

♦ Leave some free time in the day for the unexpected.

There are no hard and fast rules for planning your day; it may be a case of experimenting to see what works for you.

Similarly, the choice of a planning aid is a personal decision. Some people find a diary quite adequate, while others make use of the extra functions of a personal organiser, electronic planner or intranet system.

Personal planning aids

Diary
Record events and appointments as and when scheduled. Keep old diaries for reference.

Personal organiser
Can function as diary, address book, weekly/monthly planner, project planner, notebook.

Electronic planner
Stores names, phone numbers, appointments and personal details in a personal form.

Intranet system
Allows access by others, for example your secretary or assistant.

Source: *Adapted from Hindle* (1998)

The activities which follow will take you through the process of reviewing your time planning and the way you use your time. The result should be a clearer perspective on how you could use your time more effectively and efficiently.

Activity 15
Review your time planning

Objective

Use this activity to review the way you plan your time.

Task

1 In the table provided, write down how you currently plan your time in the medium and short term. Note any comments on how well these methods work.

2 Write down how you estimate the time that activities will take.

3 Using the information in the Time Management theme as a source of ideas, note some improvements you will try.

	Current method(s)	Improvements to try
Medium/long-term planning		
Weekly/daily planning		
Estimating the time a task will take		

Feedback

You may want to discuss any ideas for improving long-term planning with your manager.

Your daily plans are a more personal affair, but your colleagues may have ideas to share.

Activity 16
Analyse your use of time

Objective

Use this activity to analyse the way you use your time.

If you are not sure how your time is being used, keeping a time log will help you. You may want to keep a general log of all your time to see how it is divided up between activities.

On the other hand, you may want to explore specific aspects of your use of time, such as:

◆ time spent on specific projects/tasks

◆ time spent on particular activities, for example reading/ e-mail/phone

◆ when you are in control (proactive time) and when you have to respond to others (reactive time)

◆ how realistically you estimate your time

◆ where the distractions come from

◆ your productive times of day.

Waiting for a typical week would probably mean you never get started on your time log. To be realistic, start as soon as you can, provided the week is not particularly atypical.

Task: Part 1

1 Note down your purpose for keeping a time log.

2 Use the blank proforma provided, or make up your own, to record your time over a period of three to five days.

3 Use the sample time logs to get ideas for aspects of your time you will record.

4 Keep your time log with you and complete it as frequently as possible through the day. By the end of the day, your previous perceptions of where your time went will have diverged from reality.

5 As each day is completed, total the number of hours in each column.

Purpose(s) for my time log:

Date:

																					Notes
Total hours																					
08.00–08.30																					
08.30–09.00																					
09.00–09.30																					
09.30–10.00																					
10.00–10.30																					
10.30–11.00																					
11.00–11.30																					
11.30–12.00																					
12.00–12.30																					
12.30–13.00																					
13.00–13.30																					
13.30–14.00																					
14.00–14.30																					
14.30–15.00																					
15.00–15.30																					
15.30–16.00																					
16.00–16.30																					
16.30–17.00																					
17.00–17.30																					
17.30–18.00																					

Sample extracts from time logs kept for the same time period for different purposes

1 To identify how time is distributed between types of work.

Purpose(s) for my time log:

Date: 8.1.04 **Activity**

Total hours	Paperwork	Phone 0.5	Computing 1.5	Planning	Travel	Meetings	Other 1	Interruptions									Notes
08.00–08.30							x										Chatting
08.30–09.00			x														E-mails
09.00–09.30		x															Phone calls
09.30–10.00			x														Design – Link project
10.00–10.30			x														Design – Link project
10.30–11.00							x										Tea & chat with Mick

2 To find out how time is distributed between areas of the job.

Purpose(s) for my time log:

Date: 8.1.04 **Job area**

Total hours	Intranet maint.	Web design	Link project 1.5	New database	Admin 0.5	Team 0.5	Other 0.5									Notes
08.00–08.30						x										Chatting
08.30–09.00					x											E-mails
09.00–09.30			x													Phone calls
09.30–10.00			x													Design – Link project
10.00–10.30			x													Design – Link project
10.30–11.00							x									Tea & chat with Mick

3 To find out how much time is proactive/reactive, and also how much time is spent on interruptions.

Note: two entries are required for periods spent dealing with interruptions.

Purpose(s) for my time log:																		
Date: **8.1.04**	Proactive/reactive							Interruptions									Notes	
Total hours	1.5	1.5							1									
	Proactive tasks	Reactive tasks						Reactive tasks										
08.00–08.30		x						x									Chatting	
08.30–09.00		x															E-mails	
09.00–09.30	x																Phone calls	
09.30–10.00	x																Design – Link project	
10.00–10.30	x																Design – Link project	
10.30–11.00		x						x									Tea & chat with Mick	

Task: Part 2

At the end of the period, reflect on the totals and decide on any changes you want to make in your use of time.

For example, focus more on proactive tasks and aim to halve the time spent on reactive tasks (often interruptions).

Conclusions from my time log:
Action I will take to improve my use of time:

Feedback

Your findings could have a variety of implications. These may relate primarily to your personal use of time, for example not allowing yourself to be distracted so much by others. On the other hand, if you find you are spending a lot of time on tasks that do not contribute to your work goals, you may need to consult others, perhaps your manager or colleagues, about dropping some of these tasks, or you may need to review your work goals.

◆ Recap

This theme has looked at managing your time.

◆ **Identify the benefits you would like to achieve by managing your time**
You may have identified that you would like to spend less time firefighting, work less hours, reduce stress levels, focus on the things that matter, be able to see complex issues more clearly.

◆ **Define and prioritise your work objectives/goals**
Goals should form a hierarchy, with the organisation's mission at the top and goals and objectives from the various levels all feeding upwards into the next level. Your priorities should be based on importance and urgency or fall into the category of critical tasks or tasks that contribute to performance.

◆ **Use planning to support you in achieving your objectives**
Making long-term, weekly and daily plans will ensure that you have a clear sense of direction and will be able to beat procrastination, capitalise on your prime time and manage distractions. There are a number of suggestions for planning aids that will support you in achieving your objectives.

 **More @**

Adair, J. (1988) *Effective Time Management*, **Pan**
In this classic guide, John Adair focuses on the time available for daily use by using a wide range of examples and case studies, helping to: identify long-term goals and middle-term plans; plan the day and make the best use of your time; and learn to delegate and acquire time effectiveness in the office and at meetings.

Forster, M. (2000) *Get Everything Done and Still have Time to Play*, **Hodder & Stoughton**
Forster is a life coach who shares his own 'attention focusing' techniques. These include looking beyond the immediate tasks, learning to say 'no', sorting out the significant from the trivial, and costing everything you do against a notional hourly rate of pay so that you can evaluate every activity against its 'cost'. He considers that the main reason most people don't do things is resistance – not lack of time.

Caunt, J. (2000) *Organise Yourself*, **Kogan Page**
Being organised means being clear about priorities and being able to manage time, people, paper and technology effectively, in order to deliver the results on which you will be judged. *Organise Yourself* offers a guide to improving all aspects of personal organisation, including: determining goals and priorities; managing time; developing new work habits; improving decision making; working with others; organising reading and paperwork; using technology productively; organising office space; and maintaining effective filing systems.

www.mindtools.com/pages/main/newMN_HTE.htm
Mindtools is a really practical and interesting website which offers articles on tools and ideas for helping you to manage your time better, such as:

- Costing Your Time – Finding out how much your time costs
- Deciding Work Priorities – Doing tasks which add the greatest value
- Activity Logs – Understanding where you lose time
- Small-Scale Planning – Action Plans
- Prioritized To Do Lists – Doing the most important things first
- Personal Goal Setting – Planning to Live Your Life Your Way
- Scheduling Skills – Planning to make the most of your time

Full references are provided at the end of the book.

5   Stress and life balance

Stress often has a negative connotation as something to be avoided because it makes us feel unwell and can lead to serious illness. Such attitudes show a lack of understanding of stress, because it also has positive aspects. We need a certain level of stress to motivate us to get on and do things. This theme aims to provide an understanding of stress that can be used to help with stress management.

Recognising where stress comes from, and knowing how you personally react to unhealthy stress, is the foundation for managing your stress more effectively. Once you have identified your stressors, and recognised the way you respond to stress, you will be in a position to consider the various ways of managing stress to your advantage.

A key challenge for many managers is how to balance the often-competing demands of home and work. It's all too easy to become consumed with one aspect of our lives at the expense of the other, resulting in stress and its associated symptoms. Here we look first at the 'big picture' of balancing your life as a whole, and then focus on more specific ways of maintaining the balance between home and work.

This theme reviews how you can balance the effects of stress, work and home life. You will:

◆ **Identify your immediate response to a stressful situation and your sources of stress**

◆ **Explore ways to minimise the effects of stress**

◆ **Explore ways to achieve overall balance in your life.**

Understanding stress

The traditional stress curve (see Figure 5.1) shows three levels of stress: understress, healthy stress and overstress.

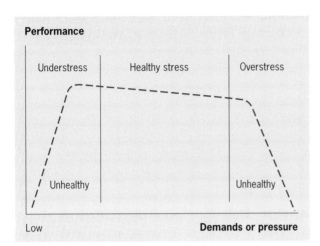

Figure 5.1 *The stress curve*   Source: *Warren and Toll* (1997)

Understress
When we feel too little stress because we have no demands or pressures on us to act, we feel lethargic and demotivated. This may be the reason unemployed people find it difficult to get up in the morning. The phrase 'I work best under pressure' acknowledges the need to have pressure to act.
As the pressure rises, we gain energy and move into the area of healthy stress.

Healthy stress
In this area we have high energy in response to the demands made of us. Our performance level rises up to a peak. At this point we feel 'stimulated, excited and challenged by the opportunities presented by a demand, appropriately in control, and with the right amount of variety of change for us'. (Warren and Toll, 1997).

Overstress
When the pressure increases further, or continues for too long, we start to become overstretched, and performance decreases. At this point we feel the demands are too great, leading to physical, mental and behavioural changes.

Occasionally, moving into overstress, perhaps for a few hours to meet a deadline, will not be harmful. The danger comes when overstress becomes prolonged and we are no longer able to cope.

Since we all have a unique way of responding to stress, the shape of the stress curve varies for each person. Finding out the shape of your stress curve, and the different points at which you operate on it, will help you to manage your stress.

85

The stress response

Hans Selye is known as the father of stress research since much of our understanding of how stress operates still draws on his 1946 'general adaptation syndrome' theory. Selye identified three stages of response to a stressful situation: alarm, resistance and exhaustion.

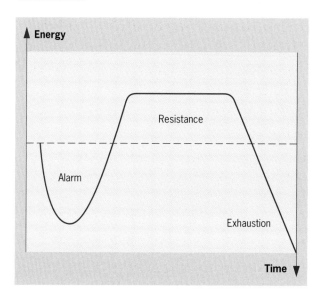

Figure 5.2 *Selye's general adaptation response*   Source: *Selye* (1946)

Livingston Booth (1985) describes these stages in Table 5.1.

Stage	Response	Effects on performance
Alarm Mobilising energy	**Self-generated response** A 'Fight or flight' Automatic response to danger, for example, being chased by a bull	Speed, power and energy well above normal
	B 'I want to' Conscious demand for energy, for example, to catch a bus or meet a deadline	Energetic, exhilarated, quickened action, can stay awake and alert to finish the job
Resistance Consuming energy	**Imposed response** C 'I have to' Imposed needs, for example, commuting, heavy workload	High energy and function, but declines if prolonged
	D 'I can't escape from', for example, caring for a handicapped relative	Irritability, over-reaction to trifles
Exhaustion Draining energy	**Distress and illness** E 'I am suffering from stress'	Function slows down, memory and concentration loss, personality changes

Table 5.1 *The stress response*   Source: *Adapted from Livingston Booth* (1985)

Being in the alarm stage is fine for a while so long as it is short term and followed by exercise or relaxation to allow the body and mind to rebalance.

Being in the resistance stage has to be accompanied by regular recreation, relaxation and rest if it is not to become harmful. It is in this stage that we have the opportunity to match the stress with our ability to cope by increasing our level of 'stress fitness'.

Being in the exhaustion stage eventually leads to chronic illness.

Bodily reactions to the alarm stage

Animals respond to the alarm of acute stress by fighting or fleeing. This is known as the 'fight or flight' response.

When the brain receives the alarm signal, messages are sent via the nerves to the muscles and organs to prepare to fight or flee. Physiological changes may include:

◆ muscles tense for action

◆ heart rate increases (for some people, anticipation of an unpleasant thing slows the heart rate)

◆ blood pressure rises

◆ sweating increases

◆ saliva dries up

◆ intestines churn and gurgle

◆ urge for bowel and bladder action.

If the state of arousal continues, hormone changes, mainly the release of adrenaline, reinforce the bodily reactions. In addition, adrenaline mobilises energy stored in the liver, making glucose available as an immediate source of energy.

The emphasis of these changes varies between individuals: for one person the increased heart rate is predominant, with little sweating, for another the main response is increased gastric activity and for another, increased muscle tension, etc.

For humans, the difficulty is that we respond in a physical way to a stimulus which usually has an emotional cause. While animals use up the physical energy produced by the stress response, for humans it is rarely appropriate to fight or run away.

Consequently we end up going through a series of immediate physiological changes which are not put to their intended use.

The effects of unhealthy stress

Physiological effects of overstress

In his book *The Joy Of Stress* (1986), Dr Hanson carries this theme of an inappropriate response forward by explaining the effects of prolonged stress (see Table 5.2).

Understanding this range of adverse consequences reinforces the need for us all to learn to manage our stress.

Stress response	Original benefit	Some of today's possible consequences
Release of cortisone	Protection from an instant allergy reaction which the 'enemy' might produce	Weakens the body's lymphatic system (which protects against infection). Reduces the stomach's resistance to its own acid
Increase in thyroid hormones	Speeds up metabolism to produce extra energy	Weight loss and insomnia
Increase of endorphins	Alleviates pain	Aggravates migraines, headaches, backache and arthritis
Reduction in sex hormones	Focuses energy on the task	Decreased libido
Shutdown of the digestive tract	Blood diverted to the key organs: muscles, heart and lungs. Mouth dries, and rectum and bladder empty	Dry mouth commonly inhibits public speaking
Sugar released into the blood, along with insulin	Provides quick burst of energy	Excessive demand for insulin may aggravate or cause diabetes. Prompts the need for a quick sugar fix
Increase in cholesterol, mainly from the liver	Helps transport fuel as the stomach has shut down. Takes over from blood sugar in supplying energy to muscles	Hardening of arteries
Racing heartbeat	Pumps more fuel-carrying blood to the vital organs	High blood pressure
Increased air supply	Dilated air passages and faster breathing provides extra oxygen to feed increased blood supply	Breathe in more pollutants, for example, cigarette smoke
The blood thickens	More capacity to carry oxygen, fight infections and stop bleeding	Encourages strokes, heart attacks, embolism
Skin 'crawls', pales and sweats	Stand-up hair makes you look bigger, blood drawn from surface for protection against cuts, sweat cools the body	Antisocial!
All five senses become acute	Brings body to peak function	High error rate after excessive stresses. The senses become less efficient

Table 5.2 *Today's drawbacks of prolonged stress response*

Source: *Derived from Hanson* (1986)

The general effects of overstress

Cooper (1981) explains that Selye's model used the idea of a simple stimulus-response approach, whereas in reality other factors, including the environment and the individual's attitude, come into play.

Taking into account this wider range of factors, Warren and Toll (1997) note that too much stress at the personal level can lead to:

◆ time off work

◆ disease

◆ mental health problems

◆ drug abuse

◆ alcoholism

- fractured relationships
- career stagnation
- boredom
- dissatisfaction
- unhappiness.

On the other hand, as Arroba and James (1987) suggest, too little stress can lead to:

- low energy and activity level
- boredom
- stodginess
- little to look forward to.

Authors variously report that between 50 per cent (Klarreich, 1988) and 75 per cent (Cooper, 1981) of all medical complaints are stress-related. Increasingly organisations are taking steps to manage the stress in the workplace and help employees to manage their own stress. If you are concerned about your health or your stress level, contact your doctor or your work counsellor.

Activity 17
Describe your stress response

Objective

This activity will help you to describe your immediate response to a stressful situation.

A stressful event causes physiological changes in the body. We each have our own response. Being aware of your response means you can easily recognise when the stress is starting, and take steps to minimise its impact.

Task

1 Using the example provided as a prompt, write down three situations that, on reflection, caused you to feel immediate stress.

2 For each one, use the checklist provided to help you and note the physiological changes that took place, for example sweating.

3 Also note any feelings you remember.

Checklist of obvious bodily reactions to stress:

☐ muscles become tense

☐ heart rate increases

☐ blood pressure rises

☐ sweating increases

☐ saliva dries up

☐ intestines churn and gurgle

☐ urge for bowel and bladder action.

Situation	My physiological response	Thoughts/feelings
Being asked to give the project's presentation	Dry mouth, butterflies, sweaty hands	I don't want to do this
1		
2		
3		

Feedback

1 When you feel these changes in future, recognise you are in a stressful situation. Start to identify the situations that give you these feelings.

2 If you can't use the physical energy generated by the stress response at the time, be sure to use it constructively later in the day.

3 When you find yourself in a stressful situation, try to decrease its effects by moving, stretching or asking yourself whether the issue will matter this time next week/year.

Sources and symptoms of stress

The stress you experience is likely to come from a wide range of sources, including your home and social lives, your work, and your personality and deeply held thoughts. As a manager it is important to consider all these sources since, for example, stress from a home situation will probably continue to play on your mind at work.

Life in general

Life events

The most-quoted listing of life stressors is the Holmes-Rahe inventory based on research in the 1960s in the US (see Holmes and Rahe 1967). In the scale, forty-three life events are rated according to the degree of stress they incur, the strongest stressors being death of a spouse or close family member, divorce, separation or marriage, jail, personal injury or illness and loss of job.

Stressful life events include potentially joyous ones such as marriage and pregnancy. The classic, supposedly joyful, event that can cause much tension is Christmas, when extended family groups feel they must have a good time.

The positive life events in the scale are marriage, marital reconciliation, retirement, pregnancy, gaining a new family member, outstanding personal achievement, vacation and Christmas.

Cooper (1981) points out that while the inventory gives a general indication 'of the extent of the change stressors you are experiencing in a variety of life areas', it does not take into account a number of other important factors, namely personal capacity to cope with stress, your support systems (at work, home, etc.) and how important the event is to you.

Ongoing sources

You are probably subject to sources of ongoing stress in your general life. For example, a dual-career marriage raises all sorts of stress, including readjusting roles, limited time together, conflicting holiday times, finding out-of-school childcare, etc. Examples of areas of life in which you may experience stress and examples of stressors are given in Table 5.3, although this list is by no means exhaustive.

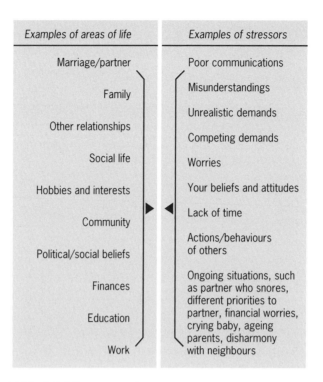

Examples of areas of life	Examples of stressors
Marriage/partner	Poor communications
Family	Misunderstandings
Other relationships	Unrealistic demands
	Competing demands
Social life	Worries
Hobbies and interests	Your beliefs and attitudes
Community	Lack of time
Political/social beliefs	Actions/behaviours of others
Finances	Ongoing situations, such as partner who snores, different priorities to partner, financial worries, crying baby, ageing parents, disharmony with neighbours
Education	
Work	

Table 5.3 *Life events and stressors*

Work

Just as there is a wide variety of sources of stress in life in general, so there are many potential sources of stress attached to work. The Consumers' Association (1988) reports that studies have identified five key sources. These are listed in Table 5.4, with examples from Arroba and James (1987).

Key sources	Examples
1 Factors intrinsic to the job	Nature of work, overload/underload, specific demands in job, extent of decision making
	Level of involvement, job satisfaction, variety and pace of work
	Workplace environment and conditions
	Travel
	Rewards: pay, appraisal, acknowledgement
2 Role in the organisation	Clear/vague boundaries, shared/conflicting expectations, clarity of job description, extent of responsibility clear or not
	Belief in the business, any conflict with values/methods
3 Career prospects	Career development, promotion, fear of redundancy, retirement, relocation, organisation's view of career path, thwarted ambition, extent of influence, job security/insecurity

Key sources	Examples
4 Relations within the organisation	Colleagues, manager, subordinates, people in the organisation, people who influence our careers, those we need to do our job
	Manager: how he or she manages you, approachable or not, his or her own stress levels
	Culture: expected behaviour, extent of communication and consultation, internal politics and power relationships, management style, organisation's level of stress
	Change: confusion about new technology, expansion, diversification, slimming down
5 The home/work interface	Conflicting demands, one interfering with the other, time constraints, life events

Table 5.4 *Checklist of pressure points at work*

Source: *Adapted from Warren and Toll* (1997)

There is one other major source of stress, which can apply to life in general or more particularly to work: yourself.

Yourself

According to a Chinese proverb:

> Two thirds of what we see is behind our eyes.

Source: *Warren and Toll* (1997)

Much of the stress we experience is caused not so much by the situation or event, but by the way we respond to it. Our own response is the aspect over which we often have most control, so it is well worth identifying the stress we cause for ourselves through our response.

Irrational thoughts

Klarreich (1988), a psychologist, claims that:

> ...illogical thinking is what manufactures stress. Normal events in the workplace are transformed by our thinking into threatening situations which can become hazardous to our well-being.

Source: *Klarreich* (1988)

In a similar vein, Arroba and James (1987) identify five common thoughts which can cause stress:

- ◆ I must do it really well
- ◆ I should do it really quickly

- ◆ I must try really hard
- ◆ I must do the job myself
- ◆ I must do things in a way that will please other people.

As these thoughts arise they generate stress, which leads to inappropriate behaviour which in turn generates more stress. Thus inappropriate thoughts can lead to a vicious cycle of stress. Of course there are many more beliefs and attitudes along these lines which can cause a stressful response.

Personality type (A/B)

In the 1950s Drs Friedman and Rosenman found that people with Type A personality, sometimes dubbed 'hurry sickness', are more likely to suffer from heart disease, a stress-related illness, than people with the more laid-back Type B personality. Therefore it is worth checking out your behaviour type (see Table 5.5). Warren and Toll (1997) call Type A and Type B behaviours 'Dasher' and 'Stroller' respectively, which neatly summarises their differences.

Type A behaviour (Dasher)	Type B behaviour (Stroller)
Never late	Casual about appointments
Very competitive	Not competitive
Anticipates what others will say	Good listener
Always rushed	Never feels rushed, even under pressure
Impatient while waiting	Can wait patiently
Goes all out	Casual
Tries to do many things at once	Takes things one at a time
Emphatic in speech	Slow deliberate talker
Wants good job recognised by others	Cares about satisfying self no matter what others think
Fast eating, walking, etc.	Slow doing things
Hard-driving	Easy-going
Hides feelings	Expresses feelings
Few interests outside work	Many outside interests
Ambitious	Satisfied with job

Table 5.5 *Characteristics of Type A and Type B behaviours*

Source: *Derived from Cooper* (1981)

In reality, most people have a mix of Type A and Type B behaviours. To complicate matters further, they may use both behaviour types in different situations, for example, sometimes being hard-driving and sometimes easy-going. So, it is important not to label yourself as one type, but rather to be aware of the different behaviours you use. All is not lost for people whose behaviour is predominantly Type A since there are ways of moving towards the more laid-back Type B behaviours.

Symptoms of unhealthy stress

An important aspect of managing stress is to be aware of the range of possible symptoms which can manifest in the physical body, in thoughts and feelings, and in behaviour. As the examples in Tables 5.6 and 5.7 show, the range of symptoms is vast.

Early physical symptoms	Thoughts and feelings	Behaviour
Headaches	Can't see the wood for the trees	Withdrawn
Over-sweating	Anxious	Irritable
Indigestion	Can't make decisions	Aggressive
Raised blood pressure	Angry	Make silly mistakes
Disturbed sleep	Upset	Smile/laugh less
Oversensitive to noise/smell	Can't concentrate	Absenteeism

Table 5.6 *Examples of symptoms of overstress*

Source: *Lomas (2000) and Consumers' Association (1988)*

Physical symptoms	Thoughts and feelings	Behaviour
Tiredness	Low self-esteem	Unreliability
Low energy	Confused thinking	Simple errors
	Lack of enthusiasm	Little interest in work
		Irregular attendance
		Moan, but no action
		Lack of decision making

Table 5.7 *Symptoms of understress*

Source: *Adapted from Warren and Toll (1997)*

Each person has a unique stress response. You can identify the symptoms you get from being overstressed or understressed and then use these signals as a warning to get in control of the stress. For overstress it is particularly important to recognise your personal early warning signs so you can take action before the pressure builds up too much.

Activity 18
Identify your sources and level of stress

Objective

Use this activity to identify your sources of work stress and gain a rough idea of your level of work stress.

Identifying where your stress comes from puts you in a position to do something about it.

Task: Part 1

1 Look through the checklist of pressure points at work.

2 Using the examples as prompts, note your own pressure points, including any others you think of which are not shown below.

Checklist of pressure points at work

Key sources	Examples	My pressure points
1 Factors intrinsic to the job	Nature of work, overload/underload, specific demands of job, extent of decision making	
	Level of involvement, job satisfaction, variety and pace of work	
	Workplace environment and conditions	
	Travel	
	Rewards: pay, appraisal, acknowledgement	
2 Role in the organisation	Clear/vague boundaries, shared/conflicting expectations, clarity of job description, extent of responsibility clear or not	
	Belief in the business, any conflict with values/methods	
3 Career prospects	Career development, promotion, fear of redundancy, retirement, relocation, organisation's view of career path, thwarted ambition, extent of influence, job security	

Key sources	Examples	My pressure points
4 Relations within the organisation	Colleagues, manager, subordinates, people in the organisation, people who influence our careers, those we need to do our job	
	Manager: how I'm managed, approachable or not, his/her own stress levels	
	Culture: expected behaviour, extent of communication and consultation, internal politics and power relationships, management style, organisation's level of stress	
	Change: confusion about new technology, expansion, diversification, slimming down	
5 The home/ work interface	Conflicting demands, one interfering with the other, time constraints, life events	

Task: Part 2

1 In the following chart, circle the appropriate score for each pair of statements to reflect your situation.

2 Add up your total score.

Charting your work stress levels

Statement A	Rating	Statement B
1 Position too secure, path predictable and mapped out	1 2 3 4 5 6 7 8 9	Position and organisation insecure
2 Too few demands	1 2 3 4 5 6 7 8 9	Too much to do
3 Tasks too easy	1 2 3 4 5 6 7 8 9	Tasks too hard
4 Too quiet	1 2 3 4 5 6 7 8 9	Too noisy
5 Repetition and little variety	1 2 3 4 5 6 7 8 9	Too much variety
6 Boredom	1 2 3 4 5 6 7 8 9	Many different projects on the go
7 Too little travel	1 2 3 4 5 6 7 8 9	Too much travel
8 Too little progression	1 2 3 4 5 6 7 8 9	Fast career track
9 Too little influence, control or responsibility	1 2 3 4 5 6 7 8 9	Too much influence, control or responsibility
10 Too little interest or involvement in work	1 2 3 4 5 6 7 8 9	Too much interest or involvement in work
11 Over-managed	1 2 3 4 5 6 7 8 9	Under-managed
12 No commitment	1 2 3 4 5 6 7 8 9	Totally committed to work

Source: *Warren and Toll* (1997)

Feedback

Part 1

Having identified your sources of stress you can reflect whether you want to minimise some of them – or cope with them more effectively.

Part 2

The minimum score of 12 reflects extreme understress. If this is the case you need to aim to increase your positive stress, and should discuss ways of doing this with your doctor, your family or perhaps your line manager.

The maximum score of 108 reflects extreme overstress. If you have a high score you should seek help from your doctor or a counsellor to enable you to manage your stress more effectively.

A middle score of 60 reflects a healthy level of stress.

As well as your overall score, pay attention to any extreme individual scores. Are they balanced out by the overall score, or do you need to pay attention to particular sources of stress?

How to cope with stress

The various approaches to coping with stress draw on several disciplines, including traditional medicine, psychology and the complementary therapies.

The main aim is to balance your stressors and your ability to cope, which means placing yourself in the 'healthy stress' area of the stress curve.

If you are understressed, you need a new challenge to increase the stress and hence your motivation; if you are continually overstressed, you should seek professional help through a doctor or counsellor.

Most managers find themselves moving between the healthy stress and overstress areas, and therefore need to find ways to reduce the stressors and/or increase their ability to cope.

Reduce sources of stress

When the pressure exceeds your ability to cope, you probably need to remove some sources of stress. For example, someone heavily involved in outside interests might benefit by withdrawing from one for a while. At work there might be the option of withdrawing from a project or explaining the situation to your manager and requesting a reduction in workload. The ability to say 'no' is one approach to reducing the accumulation of stress.

Gross (1991) applies Pareto's law to suggest that 80 per cent of stress is caused by 20 per cent of stressors, so it is worth trying to identify those sources which generate most stress for you and find a way to remove them.

The Consumers' Association (1988) points out that removing one problem from a stressful situation frequently has a dramatic effect on the other symptoms. For example, modifying an attitude of perfectionism can lead to less stress getting the work done and also improved relationships with family and colleagues, which in turn have their own beneficial spin-offs.

Increase your stress fitness

If you feel that the gap between the demands made on you and your ability to cope is not too great, you may want to take the alternative approach of increasing your stress fitness by selecting from the following range of strategies.

It is beyond the scope of this theme to describe the strategies in detail. Before trying out a method that is new to you, such as assertiveness, improved diet, changing negative thoughts, you will need to inform yourself more fully about it. The More @ section at the end of this theme gives some starting points.

Rate your stress fitness

First, however, it is helpful to know how fit you are to deal with stress at the moment.

The Hanson Scale of Stress Resistance (see Figure 5.3) identifies, from a medical viewpoint, ten factors which can weaken and ten factors which can strengthen your resistance to stress. It gives a very rough indication of your resistance.

Weak choices	Score	Strong choices	Score
Poor genetics (parents/grandparents died before 65 yrs)	−10	Good genetics (parents/grandparents outlived 65 years)	10
Insomnia	−20	Sense of humour	20
Poor diet	−30	Good diet	30
Obesity	−40	Alternate your stresses	40
Unrealistic goals	−50	Realistic goals	50
Poisons: excess alcohol, tranquillisers, caffeine	−60	Understanding of stress	60
Smoking	−70	Relaxation skills and efficient sleep	70
Wrong job	−80	Thorough job preparation	80
Financial distress	−90	Financial security	90
Unstable home	−100	Stable home	100

Figure 5.3 *Hanson Scale of Stress Resistance*   Source: *Hanson* (1986)

Identifying your weaknesses should help steer you towards appropriate methods of increasing your stress fitness.

Quick fix

One way of dealing with minor stresses is to dissipate the tension they bring at the time or very quickly after the event. Lomas (2000) suggests several methods, including:

♦ take three deep breaths

♦ stretch or walk

♦ ask yourself if the issue will matter at all next week/month.

Making one of these methods a habit can go a long way to preventing the accumulation of stress through the day.

Improve your lifestyle

Increasing your stress fitness will give you more capacity to cope with existing stresses and new ones which come along. This is mainly achieved through a healthy lifestyle, which has been well promoted by the media in recent years. In summary, it involves:

♦ relaxation – through the day, for example, power nap

♦ regular deep relaxation, for example, meditation, massage, reflexology, tai chi

♦ exercise – three sessions a week in which the heartbeat is raised for twenty minutes, for example, walking, swimming, dancing, sports, gym, etc.

♦ good diet – fresh fruit and vegetables daily, low salt, low saturated fats, low sugar, plenty of fibre, variety of foods to ensure intake of vitamins and minerals.

Beware, however, of becoming obsessed about your health. Some people have taken nutrition and the gym to extremes and ended up increasing rather than decreasing their stress.

> Warren and Toll (1997) add two further aspects to stress fitness:
>
> ◆ talking, for example, to explore problems, express feelings, reflect
>
> ◆ interests – from crosswords through voluntary work to theatre.

Most managers are probably aware of these aspects of healthy living, so why do many not put them into practice? Arroba and James (1987) suggest we have many beliefs which stop us giving ourselves permission to devote time and attention to ourselves. For example, 'Looking after myself is selfish' needs to be turned round to the more helpful message, 'Looking after myself is sensible'. Women often put others first, sometimes to the point of breakdown, whereas recognising the need to look after themselves and thereby keep healthy actually puts them in a stronger position to help others.

Minimise the stress you cause yourself

In a similar vein, the way we respond to a stressful situation affects the level of stress it causes. Learning to change negative thoughts (inappropriate inner dialogue) to positive thoughts (appropriate inner dialogue) is the basis of assertive behaviour.

Change damaging beliefs and thoughts

Changing beliefs and thoughts involves:

◆ identifying inappropriate beliefs and thoughts

◆ after a stressful event, reflecting on the thoughts that went through your head, and writing down any which were inappropriate

◆ finding a more appropriate belief/response (see Table 5.8 for some examples)

◆ writing your ideas down – aim for 'win-win' thinking

◆ embedding the new thinking.

Repeat your appropriate belief/thought to yourself on a daily basis. Put the written version in a place where you will see it often.

Changing the beliefs of a lifetime does not happen overnight; the key is to be persistent in repeating the new belief to yourself until it takes over from the old one.

Inappropriate belief/thought	Appropriate belief/thought
I must not make mistakes	I can make mistakes, try to correct them and learn from them
I must be in control all the time	I give myself the right to be out of control once in a while
Why is she letting me down again?	She has different priorities to me. That's OK. I'll find a way of solving this so we both feel OK
I'm going to have to complain to the software company again – they're late again and the training is still below standard	I need to meet their director and renegotiate our contract for software support

Table 5.8 *Examples of changed beliefs and thoughts*

Source: *Derived from Warren and Toll* (1997)

Arroba and James (1987) *and Klarreich* (1988)

Modify Type A behaviour

Here are some tips for modifying Type A behaviour towards the more laid-back Type B behaviour:

◆ Do more listening than talking

◆ Avoid making unnecessary appointments and unrealistic deadlines

◆ Recognise your hurry and take steps to slow down, for example, purposefully go to a restaurant where you know you will have to wait

◆ Take time to think about the best way to approach a task before starting

◆ Learn to say 'no' to protect your time

◆ Introduce periods of reflection to identify the root causes of your 'hurry sickness'

◆ Develop stress-free breathing spaces during the day to take the pressure off the immediate task and create opportunities for complete relaxation.

Source: *Derived from Cooper* (1981) *and Friedman and Rosenman* (1974)

Find and use support

Talking over problems and sharing worries is a positive step in reducing stress...Sometimes just putting fears or emotions into words makes them clearer and more easy to come to terms with, or makes it possible to see difficulties in their proper perspective.

Source: *Consumers' Association* (1988)

Research evidence (cited in Cooper 1981) confirms that support from the individual's work group and social group can offset the effects of stress.

Sources of support can be:

◆ informal – friends, colleagues, partner, family, extended family, informal networks

◆ professional – personnel or counselling staff at work, outside experts, for example general practitioner, psychotherapist, Citizens' Advice Bureau.

For some situations, the more neutral the person, the more useful they can be. For example, a close colleague may be too enmeshed with your position to put it in perspective, and a close friend may be too involved to help with a relationship problem.

Once you have identified some actions to take to manage your stress better, use your support network to help you make the changes and keep you motivated.

Activity 19
Minimise self-induced stress

Objectives

There are two parts to this activity. Plan to complete them both to:

◆ identify the stress you cause yourself

◆ identify ways to minimise the effects of these sources of stress.

There are two main ways you can cause stress for yourself:

◆ through your thoughts and beliefs

◆ through your personality type.

Task: Part 1

1 Look through the list of five inappropriate beliefs that commonly cause stress.

2 Note down those that apply to you.

3 Think about situations which cause you stress (your work on previous activities should help here), and particularly the thoughts which went through your mind at the time of the event, or afterwards.

4 Note down any further thoughts or beliefs that could be turned into more positive ones and hence minimise your stress.

103

Five inappropriate beliefs:

◆ You must do it really well

◆ You must do it really quickly

◆ You must try really hard

◆ You must do the job yourself

◆ You must do things in a way that will please other people.

Inappropriate belief	Appropriate belief
I must not make mistakes	I can make mistakes and try to correct them

Task: Part 2

1 This section will help you identify whether your behaviour tends towards Type A or Type B.

2 In the following table, circle the number that most closely represents your own behaviour.

	Statement A	Rating	Statement B
1	Never late	5 4 3 2 1 0	Casual about appointments
2	Very competitive	5 4 3 2 1 0	Not competitive
3	Anticipates what others will say	5 4 3 2 1 0	Good listener
4	Always rushed	5 4 3 2 1 0	Never feels rushed, even under pressure
5	Impatient while waiting	5 4 3 2 1 0	Can wait patiently
6	Goes all out	5 4 3 2 1 0	Casual
7	Tries to do many things at once	5 4 3 2 1 0	Takes things one at a time
8	Emphatic in speech	5 4 3 2 1 0	Slow deliberate talker
9	Wants good job recognised by others	5 4 3 2 1 0	Cares about satisfying self no matter what others think
10	Fast eating, walking etc.	5 4 3 2 1 0	Slow doing things
11	Hard-driving	5 4 3 2 1 0	Easy-going
12	Hides feelings	5 4 3 2 1 0	Expresses feelings
13	Few interests outside work	5 4 3 2 1 0	Many outside interests
14	Ambitious	5 4 3 2 1 0	Satisfied with job

Feedback

Part 1

It takes effort to embed more appropriate beliefs into your mind. Try repeating them to yourself at regular times, for example in the shower, or writing them on a card and sticking it on the fridge or mirror. The effort will pay off as your appropriate beliefs should take away some of your stress.

Part 2

High scores reflect Type A behaviour, sometimes known as 'hurry sickness'; low scores reflect the more laid-back Type B behaviour.

The following list suggests some ways of modifying Type A behaviour:

◆ Do more listening than talking

◆ Avoid making unnecessary appointments and unrealistic deadlines

◆ Recognise your hurry, and take steps to slow down, for example purposefully go to a restaurant where you know you will have to wait

◆ Take time to think about the best way to approach a task before starting

◆ Learn to say 'no' to protect your time

◆ Introduce periods of reflection to identify the root causes of your 'hurry sickness'

◆ Develop stress-free 'breathing spaces' during the day to take the pressure off the immediate task, and make opportunities for complete relaxation.

Activity 20
Increase your stress fitness

Objectives

Use this activity to:

◆ assess your stress fitness level

◆ identify steps you will take to improve it.

This activity is in two parts. Part 1 enables you to assess your resistance to stress; Part 2 is about planning any improvements.

Hanson's rating gives a very rough indication of your current stress fitness. It will help you pinpoint which aspects of your lifestyle you need to improve to make you resistant to stress.

Task: Part 1

1 Look at the lists of strong and weak choices in the tables that follow, and circle the one that best describes you.

2 Add up your score for weak choices and strong choices.

The Hanson Scale of Stress Resistance

Weak choices	Score	Strong choices	Score
Poor genetics (parents/grandparents died before 65 yrs)	−10	Good genetics (parents/grandparents outlived 65 years)	10
Insomnia	−20	Sense of humour	20
Poor diet	−30	Good diet	30
Obesity	−40	Alternate your stresses	40
Unrealistic goals	−50	Realistic goals	50
Poisons: excess alcohol, tranquillisers, caffeine	−60	Understanding of stress	60
Smoking	−70	Relaxation skills and efficient sleep	70
Wrong job	−80	Thorough job preparation	80
Financial distress	−90	Financial security	90
Unstable home	−−100	Stable home	100
Score		Score	

Source: *Hanson* (1986)

Task: Part 2

Use the results from Part 1 of this activity, the reminder below and your general knowledge to identify aspects of your lifestyle you need to improve, and list some steps you will take.

Key aspects of a healthy lifestyle

◆ Relaxation
Through the day, e.g. power nap
Regular deep relaxation, e.g. meditation, massage, reflexology, tai chi

◆ Exercise
Three sessions a week in which the heartbeat is raised for twenty minutes, e.g. walking, swimming, dancing, sports, gym

◆ Good diet
Fresh fruit and vegetables daily, low salt, low saturated fats, low sugar, plenty of fibre, variety of foods to ensure intake of vitamins and minerals.

Aspects of my lifestyle I need to improve	Action I will take

Feedback

Part 1

Your score will be in the range: –550 for a very weak lifestyle to 550 for a very healthy lifestyle.

Working through these pairs should have helped you to identify aspects of your lifestyle you need to improve. This will help with Part 2 of this activity.

Part 2

Identifying the action you will take is a major step towards increasing your resistance to stress. This activity may well have prompted you to write down the action that you have known for a while you need to take. The next step is to take it. Here are some tips:

♦ Be realistic in your plans

♦ Start in a small way and build up

♦ Involve other people in your plans – that way you are more likely to keep going.

Balancing home and work

Here are some common home/work conflicts managers may experience:

◆ feeling guilty about not being at home to look after the children

◆ resenting not spending enough time with the family

◆ missing out on social life from working overlong hours

◆ demands of dependent relatives conflicting with work responsibilities

◆ not earning enough to meet expenses/satisfy a preferred lifestyle

◆ expecting to fulfil both home and work roles to perfection.

You probably have others to add to the list. Reviewing the balance of your life, and in some cases modifying your beliefs, should help you to move towards resolving such conflicts.

Find an overall balance

Before we can think about ways to balance home and work, we need to review our lives. The following methods help to answer three key questions:

◆ What are you aiming to achieve with your life?

◆ How satisfied are you with different aspects of your life?

◆ How is your time currently distributed between different aspects of your life?

What do you want to achieve?

Experts suggest writing your eulogy as a way of thinking about what you really want to achieve with your life, and how you want to live it – see Covey (1992) and Charlesworth and Nathan (1987).

How to write your eulogy

Find a quiet time when you will not be disturbed, imagine yourself at your own funeral attended by friends and relatives and think what you would like four speakers to say about your life. The speakers are a family member, a friend, someone from work and someone from a community organisation or church.

What would you want them to say about you as a person, your contributions, your achievements, the difference you made to their lives?

Write down your thoughts.

> This experience is a good antidote to the detail of everyday living. It forces you to think about what you really want to achieve with your life.

Source: *Covey* (1992)

These thoughts can form the basis for writing your life goals.

How satisfied are you with aspects of your life?

As part of the *Mindstore* mental fitness programme, Jack Black (1994) uses the 'wheel of life' to help people rate their satisfaction with eight aspects of life. For each aspect you give yourself a score of 1–10, where 10 indicates this aspect of your life is perfect, and 1 indicates that you are highly dissatisfied with this aspect.

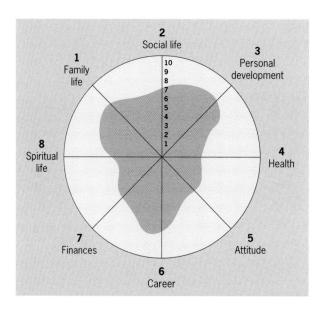

Figure 5.4 *Example of a filled-in wheel of life*

Source: *Adapted from Black* (1994)

The example shown in Figure 5.4 is typical – the person is satisfied with some areas of her life, but very dissatisfied with others. To lead a more balanced life, she needs to focus more attention on the areas with which she is dissatisfied.

Where does your time go?

Warren and Toll (1997) quote research findings that British males work longer hours than European males, with some working more than eight hours longer than the EC (European Community) recommended maximum of forty-eight hours a week. They also quote Cooper and Sutherland's finding (2000) that the optimal working week is between thirty-five and forty-five hours, and that many chief executives want to achieve a better balance between work and home/family.

Achieving a balance between work and home is not possible if work dominates our use of time. Ways to reduce the time spent working include:

◆ focusing clearly on work which contributes to work goals

◆ improving efficiency using time and stress-management techniques

◆ considering a career adjustment, such as renegotiated workload, job share, career break.

Source: *Derived from Gross* (1991)

Drawing a pie chart, as shown in Figure 5.5, can help you review the time you spend at work in relation to other aspects of your life.

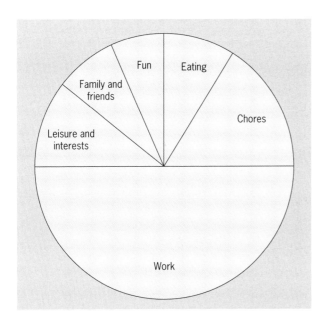

Figure 5.5 *A time pie*   Source: *Warren and Toll* (1997)

Consider whether the segments are in the right proportion. If not, how do you want to change them? You could draw a second pie chart showing your life as you would like it to be.

Tying it all together

Using these three methods, you can:

◆ write your life goals for the next five years, and prioritise them

◆ identify areas of your life you want to give more/less attention

◆ identify how you want to distribute your time between the various aspects of your life.

It's a good idea to involve those close to you when planning these life changes.

Keep the balance

Once you have defined how you want your life to be in broad terms, you can focus on the details of maintaining the balance.

Winning at home

When work predominates, it is often family life that suffers. Gross (1991) suggests that some people 'metamorphose' as they arrive home from being a creative, self-confident, cheerful and charming professional into a person who is drained. This means they have little energy to put in the effort that is needed to keep relationships with their partner and family going.

Tips for giving more attention to your home life

♦ Create a break between work and home, perhaps sitting in the car for a few minutes to relax

♦ Greet your partner/family cheerfully as your greeting sets the tone for the evening

♦ Use the same respect, courtesy, consideration and energy at home as you use at work with your colleagues and customers

♦ Treat your relationships as projects to be worked at – they flounder when left to coast along without any input

♦ Concentrate on the present moment.

A couple's monthly planning session

One couple set aside a Friday evening a month for joint planning. They refuse social invitations for that evening, and don't turn on the TV. When the kids have gone to bed they balance their chequebook and update their finances. They review their goals, and make goals and plans for the coming month. They also discuss any points of conflict or friction that seem to be developing so they can resolve them in a calm atmosphere.

Source: *Warren and Toll* (1997)

Portfolio marriages

Handy suggests that 'portfolio careers' will be matched with 'portfolio marriages' in which the roles of the partners are very flexible to meet the varying demands on their time. Marriages have traditionally evolved to adjust to the stages of child rearing, adolescence, empty nest and retirement. However, in a portfolio marriage the adjustments required are more complex as the needs of dual careers, housekeeping, family life and other interests continually change. Providing this flexibility requires an awareness of the changing roles and demands within the marriage/partnership.

Source: *Derived from Handy* (1991)

Activity 21
Review your life balance

Objectives

Use this activity to:

◆ review the current balance in your life

◆ identify ways to make your life more balanced.

Part 1 of this activity will take most time, and requires approximately half an hour of peace and quiet.

Task: Part 1

1 Write your eulogy.
2 Define some life goals for yourself.

How to write your eulogy

Find a quiet time when you will not be disturbed, imagine yourself at your own funeral attended by friends and relatives, and think what you would like four speakers to say about your life. The speakers are: a family member, a friend, someone from work, and someone from a community organisation or church.

What would you want them to say about you as a person, your contributions, your achievements and the difference you made to their lives?

Write down your thoughts.

This experience is a good antidote to the detail of everyday living. It forces you to think about what you really want to achieve with your life.

Source: *Covey* (1992)

Notes for the eulogy you'd like to have: *Ideas for life goals:*

Task: Part 2

1 Review the eight aspects of life in the wheel of life provided here. If they are not appropriate to you, change the labels or add in an extra one.

2 Think about each aspect in turn. Mark on the scale how satisfied you are with this aspect of your life, using 1 for very dissatisfied and 10 for very satisfied.

3 Join up the points you have marked.

4 Reflect on how balanced your life is, and note your conclusions in the box.

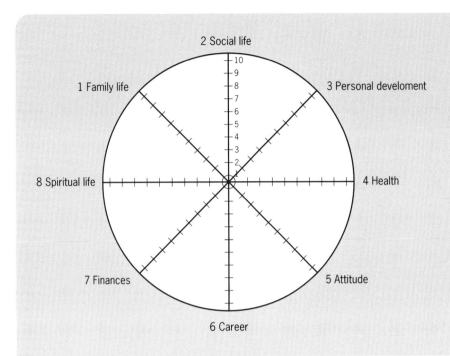

Reflections on the balance in my life:

For example: I really need to sort out our finances. I need to make my wheel more balanced.

Task: Part 3

1   Use the blank circle below to draw a pie chart of how you use your time. You could use the eight aspects from the wheel of life in the previous task, or the categories in the example provided here. You may be able to draw on your work for Activity 5 in this part of the activity.

2   Note down anything you would like to change about the way you use your time.

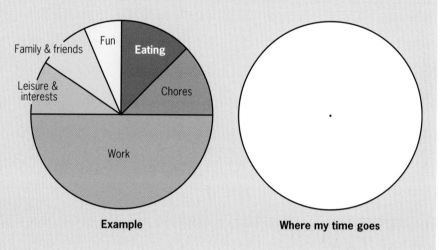

Example   **Where my time goes**

Things I would like to change about the way I use my time:

Task: Part 4

1   Review the first three parts of this activity and reflect on the results.

2   Consider the main changes you want to make to the balance of your life, and identify the first three steps you will take.

Main changes I will make to achieve a better balance in my life:	First three steps

Feedback

Part 1

You probably found that activity challenging since it forced you to look at the big picture of your life. It may be an activity you want to return to.

Don't worry if your goals are not too specific at this stage. The important thing is to start working on them. To be effective you need to be continually aware of them, so they should evolve naturally.

Part 2

Is your wheel fairly smooth or, as most people's tend to be, rather 'jagged'?

This part should have helped you identify aspects of your life that are receiving too much or too little attention. The next part will bring this into sharper focus.

Parts 3 and 4

Reviewing the whole of your life is a big job! You have probably realised that it will be an ongoing task, and needs to involve those close to you. It would be a good idea to revisit this type of activity so that you move periodically from the detail of day-to-day living to this kind of 'helicopter view'.

◆ Recap

◆ **Identify your immediate response to a stressful situation and your sources of stress**
It is important to understand the psychological and physiological effects of stress so that you can identify the symptoms and source of your stress and do something about it.

◆ **Explore ways to minimise the effects of stress**
This theme examines the importance of stress fitness, improving your lifestyle, changing damaging thoughts and beliefs, and finding and using support.

◆ **Explore ways to achieve overall balance in your life**
Reviewing the balance of your life, and in some cases modifying your beliefs, should help you to move towards resolving home/work conflicts.

▶▶ More @

Arroba, T. and James, K. (1987) Pressure at work, McGraw-Hill
This book focuses on the field of stress management and examines the holistic elements that have become accepted in the field of management development and techniques for managing stress. It also provides exercises and examples throughout.

Lomas, B. (2000) *Easy Step by Step Guide to Stress and Time Mangement*, Rowmark
This guide gives lots of tips on how to manage your time, how to take stock of your life, how to regain control of it and how to ease your stress level. It covers:

◆ How to recognise the symptoms of stress

◆ How to get more out of your working day and your life whilst managing your stress level

◆ How to prioritise both at work and at home

◆ How to say 'no' to those requests you would like to turn down

◆ How to get others to say 'yes' to taking over what you normally have to do

◆ How to diffuse stressful situations.

Warren, E. and Toll, C. (1997) *The stress workbook*, **Nicholas Brealey**

For anyone who has experienced stress at work and wants to combine high performance with a healthy lifestyle and help others to do so, this workbook provides many practical answers by focusing on the individual, the manager, the team and the organisation as a whole with a range of tried-and-tested techniques. The book dispels the popular myths, draws on current best practice and provides a straightforward guide to a topic that has vital implications for performance at work.

www.mindtools.com/pages/main/newMN_TCS.htm
Mindtools is a really practical and interesting website which offers articles on tools and ideas for helping you to manage stress, such as:

◆ Stress Diary – Identifying the short-term stress in your life

◆ Job Analysis – The first step in managing work overload and job stress

◆ Performance Planning – Planning ahead to reduce performance stress

◆ Imagery – Mental stress management

◆ Physical Relaxation Techniques – Deep breathing, PMR and the 'Relaxation Response'

◆ Thought Awareness, Rational Thinking and Positive Thinking

◆ Rest, Relaxation and Sleep – Starting to manage long-term stress

◆ Burnout Self-Test – Testing yourself to avoid burnout

References

Adair, J. (1988) *Effective time management*, Pan

Arroba, T. and James, K. (1987) *Pressure at Work*, McGraw-Hill

Austin, B. (1986), revised edition, *Making effective use of executive time*, Management Update

Benner, P. (1984) *From Novice to Expert: Excellence and Power in Clinical Nursing Practice*, Addison Wesley

Black, J. (1994) *Mindstore,* Thorsons

Bliss, E. C. (1991) revised edition, *Getting Things Done*, Warner

Caunt, J. (2000) *Organise Yourself,* Kogan Page

Charlesworth, E. A. and Nathan, R. G. (1987), *Stress management,* Corgi

Conger, J. (1998) How Generation X Managers Manage, *Strategy and Business*

Consumers' Association (1988) Understanding Stress, *Which?*

Cooper, G. L. (1981) *The Stress Check*, Spectrum

Covey, S. R. (1992) *The Seven Habits of Highly Effective People*, Simon Schuster

Crozier, W. R. (1992) *Individual learners: personality differences in education*, Routledge

Fitzgerald, M. (1994) 'Theories of Reflection for Learning' in Palmer, A., Burns, S. and Bulman, C., *Reflective Practice in Nursing*, Blackwell

Fleming, I. (1997) 4th edition, *The Time Management Pocketbook*, Management Pocketbooks Ltd

Forster, M. (2000) *Get everything done and still have time to play*, Hodder & Stoughton

Friedman, M. D. and Rosenham, R. H. (1974) *Type A Behaviour and Your Heart*, Knopf

Garratt, B. (1990) *Creating a Learning Organisation*, Director Books

Garratt, S. (1985) *Manage Your Time*, Fontana/Collins

Goleman, D. (1995) *Emotional Intelligence*, Bantam

Gross, G. F. (1991) *Win at Work and at Home*, Director Books

Guirdham, M. (1995) 2nd edition, *Interpersonal Skills at Work*, Pearson

Handy, C. (1991) *The Age of Unreason*, Random Century

Handy, C. (1993) *Understanding Organisations*, Penguin Business

Hanson, P. (1986) *The Joy of Stress*, Pan

Haynes, M. E. (1988) *Make Every Minute Count*, Crisp

Hindle, T. (1998) *Manage Your Time*, Dorling Kindersley

Holmes, T. and Rahe, R. (1967) 'Holmes-Rahe Social readjustment rating scale', *Journal of Psychometric Research*, vol II

Honey, P. and Mumford, A. (1976) *The Manual of Learning Styles*, Peter Honey publications

Kakabadse, A., Ludlow, R. and Vinnicombe, S. (1987) *Working in Organisations*, Gower

Kanter, R. M. (1989) *When Giants Learn to Dance*, Simon & Schuster

Kelly, G. A. (1970) 'Behaviour is an experiment' in Banister, D. (ed), *Perspectives in Personal Construct Theory*, Academic Press

Klarreich, S. H. (1988) *The Stress Solution*, Cedar

Knasel, E. G. and Meed, J. (1994) *Becoming Competent: Effective Learning for Occupational Competence*, Department for Education and Employment

Knasel, E. G., Meed, J. and Rossetti, A. (2000) *Learn for Your Life: A Blueprint for Continuous Learning*, Financial Times Prentice Hall

Kolb, D. A. (1984) *Experiential Learning: Experience as a Source of Learning and Development*, Prentice Hall

L'Aiguille, Y. (1994) 'Pushing back the boundaries of personal experience' in Palmer, A., Burns, S. and Bulman, C., *Reflective Practice in Nursing*, Blackwell

Lakein, A. (1984) *How to get control of your time and your life*, Gower

Law, B. (1996) 'A Career-Learning Theory' in Watts, A. G., Law, B., Killeen, J., Kidd, J. M. and Hawthorn, R. *Rethinking Careers Education and Guidance*, Routledge

Livingston Booth, A. (1985) *Stressmanship*, Severn House

Lomas, B. (2000) *Easy Step by Step Guide to Stress and Time Mangement*, Rowmark

Luft, J. and Ingham, H. (1955) 'The Johari Window: A Graphic Model of Interpersonal Awareness', Proceedings of the Western Training Laboratory in Group Development, Los Angeles

Mabey, C. and Iles, P. (1994) *Managing Learning*, OUP

Myers Briggs, I. B. (1962) *The Myers Briggs Types Indicator*, Educational Testing Service, USA

O'Connor, J. and McDermott, I. (1996) *Principles of Neurolinguistic Programming*, Thorsons

Pask, G. (1988) 'Learning strategies, teaching strategies and conceptual or learning styles', in Schmeck, R. R. (Ed), *Learning Strategies and Learning Styles*, Plenum Press

Pedler, M., Burgoyne, J. and Boydell, T. (1991) *The Learning Company*, McGraw-Hill

Peters, T. (1997) 'The brand called You' in *Fast company*, 10

Peters, T. and Austin, N. (1985) *A Passion for Excellence*, Random House

Rogers, C. R. (1961) *On Becoming a Person*, Constable

Schein, E. (1970) *Organisational Psychology*, Prentice Hall

Schön, D. A. (1983) *The Reflective Practitioner: How Professionals Think in Action*, Basic Books

Schonberger, R. J. (1990) *Building a Chain of Customers*, Hutchinson

Selye, H. (1946) 'The General Adaptation Syndrome and the Diseases of Adaptation', in *Journal of Clinical Endocrinology*

Senge, P. M. (1990) *The Fifth Discipline*, Century Business

Warren, E. and Toll, C. (1997) *The Stress Workbook*, Nicholas Brealey